"I am excited about the book Bruce Howard has written. He has taken what I intuitively know to be true and written a well-documented, well-thought-out book that says, 'The American economy may not be as bad as the news media and best-selling authors would lead you to believe.' My thoughts, at best, are opinions as I am not an economist but rather a financial planner. Bruce's book is written from the perspective of an economist.

"I am delighted that this book dispels some of the myths that are prevalent in the Christian community." **Ron Blue,** financial and investment counselor

"Bruce Howard provides a reasoned and professional approach to understanding the principles of what makes our economic system work, including a full treatment of its warts and moles. He also reminds us that God has called us to think through our faith and act—not just fear and react." **C. William Pollard,** chairman of the board, ServiceMaster Corp.

"This book will enrich any Christian who seeks to understand the great blessings God has showered on America." **John M. Templeton,** chairman, Templeton Mutual Funds Group

"As reporters and politicians depress us by counting our economic problems, it will lift our spirits to reflect that this economist counts our manifold blessings." **Gary Moore,** author of *The Thoughtful Christian's Guide to Investing*

Safe AND Sound

WHY YOU CAN STAND SECURE ON THE FUTURE OF THE U.S. ECONOMY

★ ★ ★ ★ ★

BRUCE HOWARD

C.P.A., Ph.D.

Tyndale House Publishers, Inc.
WHEATON, ILLINOIS

Scripture quotations are taken from the *Holy Bible,* New International Version®. Copyright © 1973, 1978, 1984 by International Bible Society. Used by permission of Zondervan Publishing House. All rights reserved. The "NIV" and "New International Version" trademarks are registered in the United States Patent and Trademark Office by International Bible Society. Use of either trademark requires permission of International Bible Society.

Library of Congress Cataloging-in-Publication Data

Howard, Bruce, date
   Safe and sound : why you can stand secure on the future of the
U.S. economy / Bruce Howard.
     p. cm.
   Includes bibliographical references.
   ISBN 0-8423-7849-9 (pbk. : alk. paper)
    1. United States—Economic conditions—1981- 2. Capitalism—
United States. 3. Capitalism—Religious aspects—Christianity.
I. Title
HC106.8.H68   1996
330.973—dc20   95-42337

Printed in the United States of America

01 00 99 98 97 96
9   8   7   6   5   4   3   2   1

CONTENTS

FOREWORD

I REMEMBER as if it were yesterday an experience I had in the early 1980s. I was on my way to work and reflecting during the commute on the bad economic news: Inflation had reached double-digit levels, interest rates were nearing 20 percent, home mortgage rates were in the 13–15 percent category, and most economic prognosticators were predicting that by 1985 the United states would have reached a position of hyperinflation from which there would be no recovery. Our economy was being compared to the German economy of the 1920s, which ultimately collapsed because of hyperinflation.

Our clients were asking—and rightfully so—what they should do. The Christian and secular books they were reading were predicting certain economic catastrophe. The media was daily forecasting economic doom. As I was pondering these things, I asked the Lord, "What should I be telling my clients and those I speak to?"

As I exited the interstate, it was as if God opened my mind to understand that from his perspective the future was secure and that the principles he has given us in his Word for how to view wealth and how to

manage money properly were not going to change. It
didn't make any difference whether we lived in an infla-
tionary, deflationary, communistic, socialistic, or any
other type of political or economic environment. There
were still basic principles to be followed in managing
money. He was in control, not us.

Even though I knew that to be unquestionably true, I
still felt a certain amount of fear in giving that kind of
advice. Now, as I look back to the 1980s, I realize that that
time of great fear was the beginning of the most prosperous decade in my life—and probably one of the most
prosperous decades in human history for any nation.
There certainly was bad news at the beginning, but from
the vantage point of time, we realize that what people
were afraid of simply did not happen.

In my recent book *Storm Shelter*, I reviewed the last sev-
enty years, showing in ten-year segments that there has
always been bad economic news. In the early 90s it was
the decline of the dollar and trade deficits. In the 80s, as I
mentioned, it was high inflation rates and high interest
rates. In the early 70s it was the oil embargo, going off the
gold standard, and an unprecedented increase in the
prime-interest rate. In the early 60s it was a political situation: the Cuban missile crisis. In the 50s it was the Berlin
crisis, the Cold War, and other political considerations. In
the early 40s, of course, it was world war. In the early 30s
it was depression. In the early 20s, again, it was world war.
I suspect that you could go on and on back into history,
because it seems to me that there is never a time when we
look forward and say confidently, "The future is going to
be secure."

Even though we tend to look at the future through the

eyes of fear, when we look at history, we can see that America in the last fifty to one hundred years has seen unprecedented prosperity. As a matter of fact, no nation in the world has ever seen the prosperity that we have experienced in America. And yet, every best-seller on finance or the economy tends to play more to fear than to reality.

This is why I am excited about the book Bruce Howard has written. He has taken what I intuitively know to be true and has written a well-documented, well-thought-out book that says, "The American economy may not be as bad as the news media and best-selling authors would lead you to believe." My thoughts, at best, are opinions as I am not an economist but rather a financial planner. Bruce's book is written from the perspective of an economist.

I believe that we need this book in the Christian world because we are living in a time of unprecedented spiritual opportunities. It seems to me that God is at work around the world in ways that are unparalleled in history as political borders are down, technologies undreamed of only a few years ago become reality, and the wealth in the hands of North Americans alone is more than enough to fund almost any missionary endeavor that could be dreamed of. I believe that fear-based, short-term financial thinking is holding back the release of that wealth. I am delighted that this book dispels some of the myths that are prevalent in the Christian community.

Last, I am delighted to write a foreword to this book because of my personal appreciation for Bruce Howard. I first became familiar with his work through my daughter, Cynthia, who was a student of his at Wheaton

College. Additionally, my firm has had the privilege of hiring some of Bruce's former students, and they have proven to be well prepared to contribute significantly to the growth of our organization. So I can testify not only to Bruce's qualifications of training and experience but also to the practical results of his expertise. I've seen those results in my own family and in my own firm. Thanks, Bruce, for writing this book.

Ron Blue
Atlanta, Georgia

PREFACE

A MAN in Texas wonders if he should sell off his home and possessions, buy gold, move to the country, and wait for the economy to collapse.

A mission board considers an investment policy for the missionaries' retirement funds prohibiting plan assets from being invested in securities of the United States government on the grounds that the United States government is on the brink of financial ruin.

A president of a sizeable manufacturing firm returns home from a business trip to find that his house has been put up for sale by his wife, who had just the day before finished reading a "Christian" book warning of the imminent demise of the U.S. economy.

These are three examples that confirm, in my mind, the confusion prevalent among many Christians today about the state of the United States economy. I believe there is a real need to provide some balance to the apocalyptic perspective on economic issues. I don't want people to live in fear when fear is unwarranted. Christians should spend less time worrying about the remote chance of needing to survive economic calamity and get back to thinking about the more important issues of the kingdom of God.

Over the last several years, I have worked with college students trying to help them understand economic issues from a biblical perspective. Our classes are consistently overflowing—and it has nothing to do with the quality (or lack thereof) of the teacher. I have found that many people, of all ages and backgrounds, have a natural interest in economic affairs. Christians seem particularly interested in thinking and talking about economic issues. Many Christians have a love/hate (or at least an appreciate/beware) attitude toward economic activity. We appreciate God's material blessings, but worry about materialism. We see the good that can come from shared wealth, but fear the greediness of the hoarder. We want to eliminate poverty, but harbor suspicions of wealth-creating economies. We believe in hard work, but pity the person who makes a god of his or her career.

In response to these issues, I have written this book. Christians want to get a handle on how the economy works. They want to develop an understanding of how they, as Christians, should personally relate to it. Ultimately, I want to encourage Christians to think about their role in economic activity. I want Christians to support economic forces that are good and constructive. At the same time, I do not want them to unwittingly embrace a system and call it "Christian" when, in reality, it relies on principles of individualism and moral relativism.

I am aware that there are those who will disagree with my basic thesis. I should like to say that it is acceptable for Christians to have different perspectives. Truth often emerges in the context of the vigorous dialog of disagreement. We should all take full advantage of the facts at hand and make use of our powers of reasoning. And that is what I invite you to do as together we look at the current state—and the foundational principles—of the U.S. economy.

INTRODUCTION

The good old days

TO UNDERSTAND the present, it is sometimes useful to first look back. And so that is where we will begin.

I love to hear about the "good old days." I recently spent a delightful evening with my grandmother, listening to her recount many events from her past. Even though I am grown, with children of my own, I still enjoy hearing her tell the old stories. Grandma's stories weave the fabric of life as it was almost ninety years ago, growing up in a family of twelve children, six boys and six girls. My mind conjures up images of dancing and fiddle music as she speaks of how her family loved to move back the dining table after supper and dance the Virginia Reel. I can sense Grandma's great affection and esteem for her own grandmother who spent the last years of her life living with my grandmother's family. This great-great-grandmother of mine was a remarkable woman who became blind at the age of sixteen and, two years later, married the boy from the farm next door. Together they too raised a family of twelve children, six brothers and six sisters, just like my grandmother's family.

"Grandma, given the chance, would you want to go back to those good old days?" I asked her.

No. She would not go back. They *were* good days: relationships and time spent with family, friends, and people in general were all very good, but they were hard days just the same. Those were days when children died from common infectious diseases. Those were days that began at 4:30 A.M. Those were days when it was hard to keep food on the table and shoes on the children's feet, days when jobs were scarce and there were terribly dark economic depressions. Those were days when her husband would try to earn enough to sustain the family by delivering fish throughout the city of Chicago—on foot—no matter what the weather was like. "Good housing" consisted of a tiny apartment on the northwest side of town. Completing high school made you a highly educated person in society.

What can change in a hundred years? Let's just take a moment and reflect a bit on how things have changed since the year 1900.

Americans are much healthier now than they were a hundred years ago. Life expectancy in the year 1900 was 47.3 years. Ninety years later it had risen to 75.4 years. At the turn of the century, Americans had to be concerned about tuberculosis, malaria, typhoid, hepatitis, diphtheria, whooping cough, polio, and smallpox. Thanks to modern advances in medicine, the incidence of these diseases today is negligible.[1]

We are a great deal more productive than we used to be. In 1990, the total amount of goods and services produced in the U.S. on a per capita basis was five times as great as it was in 1900. People are working 30 percent fewer hours to produce five times as much as they did in

1900. The average American worked almost ten hours a day, six days a week in the year 1900. By 1990 we were working eight-hour days, five days a week.[2]

We have seen incredible changes in the way we live. Just operating a household took a great deal more time ninety years ago. In 1900 a household spent about forty-four hours a week on meal preparation and cleanup. Seven hours a week were spent on laundry, and another seven hours each week were devoted to cleaning the home. Seventy-five years later, hours spent in meal preparation and cleanup had fallen to ten hours a week, and only one hour a week was spent doing laundry. (Apparently our homes needed just as much cleaning, however, because we were still spending the same seven hours each week cleaning them in 1975 as we were in 1900!)[3]

The homes in which we live today are bigger and nicer than they were a century ago. Only 24 percent of homes had running water in 1890. Just 15 percent of houses in 1900 had flush toilets. In 1900 no homes were heated with gas or electricity. Coal was used to heat 63 percent of homes in 1908, with another 36 percent still using wood. Almost one quarter (23 percent) of American households in 1910 had more than three persons per sleeping room. By 1990, only one percent of Americans households were that crowded.[4]

Today we enjoy a wide variety of appliances in our homes that were virtually unknown just one hundred years ago. In 1900, 100 percent of Americans lived without refrigerators, washing machines, microwave ovens, air conditioners, dishwashers, garbage disposals, or freezers. By 1987, 100 percent of U.S. households had refrigerators, 73 percent had washing machines, 61 percent had microwave ovens, 62 percent had air conditioners, 43 percent had dishwashers, and 35 percent had freezers.[5]

Our ability to communicate has increased dramatically. At the turn of the century, there was only one phone for every fifty-eight people. Today there are roughly two phones for every three people. For every telephone conversation that took place in 1900, there were 160 conversations on a telephone in 1985. The first transmission of a human voice by means of radio waves didn't occur until 1906. By 1990, the average American family had two radios. Furthermore, 98 percent of households owned at least one TV, 59 percent had cable television service, and 72 percent had VCRs. By contrast, only 8 percent of dwellings even had *electricity* in 1907.

Our income now goes much further than it did a hundred years ago. To feed an average family of four in the year 1900 took almost 41 percent of the family's income. By 1990, food expenditures amounted to only 8 percent of the income for a family of four, with another 5 percent spent on dining out. Housing expenditures for a four-person family fell from 17 percent to 14 percent of income, and the amount spent on clothing decreased from 12 percent to 5 percent over this same period of time. All combined, expenditures on food, shelter, and clothing fell from 70 percent to only 32 percent of a family's income, which left a good deal more for other things.

We have experienced substantial gains in education over the last hundred years as well. At the turn of the century, only half of our children ages five to nineteen were enrolled in school. By 1990, 91.4 percent of our children were in school. And those enrolled were spending more time in school: The average number of days of primary or secondary school attended has increased from 99 to 160 days per year since 1900. Higher education has also experienced significant growth. For every one college graduate in 1900, there were thirty-five graduating from a college or university in 1990. Only 2.3 percent of young people ages eighteen to twenty-four were enrolled in college in 1900. By 1992, that percentage had increased to 32.2.[6]

They may have been good old days, but in many different ways and by many different standards, today is better. Compared to where we as a nation were a hundred years ago, most of us have it relatively good. Things will get even better. Let me show you how the strength and stability of the U.S. economy will help make that happen.

CHAPTER 1

Reasons to Believe

What's going right in the U.S. economy

IT IS my opinion that the United States is nowhere near a state of economic collapse. In many ways, things have never looked better. I will grant you that there is still plenty of room for improvement. Not all of us are enjoying "the good life" as we have come to expect it. I will also grant you that government policies and actions may hinder that path of improvement and even decrease our current standard of living. But the economy is not going to immediately collapse as a result of what any single person (or couple) in the White House does. Even Congress would have difficulty in destroying the economy. Contrary to what legislators often think, the economy is largely beyond their ability to influence in a direct and immediate fashion. It is too large and too complicated. Americans are too independent to bend to the will of a misguided Congress and too creative to totally succumb to its rules and regulations. Historically, Americans work with government only until that government quits working for them. At that point, we get a new government. Just ask King George.

It goes against our human nature to focus on what is going right. When I am sick with the stomach flu, or when I have a very bad cold or sore throat, or maybe even all of the above at the same time, I feel terrible. I'm ready to start making funeral arrangements. But my wife, a medical professional, will quickly assess my vital signs and give me her report.

"Heart is good. Lungs are good, too. Blood pressure is just fine. Neurological signs all seem to check out. Well, honey," she'll continue, "I think you're going to pull through this just fine. Please don't be such a baby!"

"Well, if I'm so healthy, how come I feel so rotten?" I respond.

You see, when we are sick, our symptoms tend to capture all of our attention. A sore throat or a stuffy head becomes our primary focus. Even though the most important bodily functions are working just fine, they escape our notice at the moment.

I think Americans often have the same reaction to the economy. You can see it in all the doom and gloom that appears on our bookshelves and in our daily papers, and in all the media attention devoted to one impending economic crisis following another. We tend to overreact to our current economic ills and behave as if they were life threatening, when in reality, we just have a bad case of the flu. Having the flu is no fun, but it is not going to kill you.

So, let's take stock of some of our economic strengths. What does the United States of America have going for it these days?

ECONOMIC OUTPUT
The United States accounts for almost one-fourth of the world's economic output. In 1992, the U.S. share of gross world product (GWP) amounted to 23 percent. Japan ac-

counted for 10 percent. It would take the combined output of Belgium, Denmark, France, Germany, Greece, Ireland, Italy, Luxembourg, the Netherlands, Portugal, Spain, and the United Kingdom to equal U.S. production in 1992.[1]

The combined sales of the top five industrial corporations in the United States in 1991 would have made the eleventh largest economy in the world. The sales of just the two largest U.S. corporations in 1991 (General Motors, $124 billion; Exxon, $103 billion) would make the list of top twenty economies as measured by gross domestic product.[2] The combined sales of General Motors, Ford Motor Corporation, and Chrysler were more than one and a half times the gross domestic output of either Sweden or Switzerland.

From 1988 to 1990 the U.S. produced on average 268 million metric tons of cereals, accounting for 14.4 percent of total world production.[3] In 1990, 43 percent of world production of corn was supplied by the U.S.[4] Agriculture has produced consistent positive trade balances since 1960. Total exports of agricultural products averaged $36 billion dollars a year over the period 1980 to 1992, producing positive trade balances averaging $16.6 billion for that same period of time.

In terms of manufactured products, over the years from 1985 to 1988 the U.S. average share of world industrial production was 5.4 percent for textiles, 3.1 percent for wood products, 11.1 percent for crude steel, 9.6 percent for paper, 18.6 percent for chemicals, and 40.8 percent for machinery.

Our persistent trade deficits in recent years have led to the false impression that U.S. exports have been declining. Exports have been increasing in real terms by 4.2 percent a year over the four-year period from 1989 to 1992.[5] The United States led the world in merchandise exports in 1992, accounting for more than 12 percent of total world exports.[6]

The U.S. exported a total of $447 billion of goods in 1992.[7] Germany was a close second with $442 billion of exports, making it virtually identical to the U.S. in terms of exporting merchandise. European countries, by virtue of their close proximity to neighboring countries, would naturally be large exporters. The same is somewhat true for the U.S. as well because a large portion of our exports of merchandise goes to Canada (21 percent in 1993) and Mexico (9 percent in 1993), who both share our borders.[8]

Japan's export performance is more remarkable considering it is an island economy and shares no borders. Japan's exports in 1992 amounted to $339 billion, about three-fourths of what was exported by the U.S. or Germany.

Even though the U.S. is a leader in exports, it is also a leader in imports, which causes us to have a trade deficit. The largest share of our imports comes from Canada. In 1993, the United States imported $111 billion in goods and services from Canada, accounting for about 21 percent of all our imports. The second largest souce of imports for the U.S. is Japan, which in 1993 accounted for another 20 percent of imports. About 7.5 percent of U.S. imports in 1993 came from Mexico.[9]

The trade deficits are the leading cause of a weaker U.S. dollar. The reason for this is that we trade dollars on the international foreign-exchange market for other currencies, like the Japanese yen and German mark, to pay for our imports. And remember, when the supply of something being sold increases, its price will fall. As we sell more and more dollars, the dollar will depreciate in value against foreign currencies. This is terrific news for the export businesses of the United States. It means the prices of U.S.–made products appear cheaper to foreign buyers because it takes less of their own currency to get dollars to pay for the goods made in the United States. A weak dollar makes imports more expensive for U.S. citizens, providing a good incentive to buy goods made in the United States. The weak dollar will do more to reduce or even eliminate the trade deficits than anything else.

Because of the sheer magnitude of the numbers, it is difficult to grasp the significance of total economic output in a way that is meaningful to us as individuals. For that reason, it is useful to analyze output on a per capita basis. Per capita comparisons between countries are tricky because goods and services have different relative prices in each country. Comparisons are also muddied by the variability of exchange rates. Nevertheless, adjustments can be made using measures of purchasing power parities (PPPs) to reflect real differences in the value of goods and services produced.

Living standards in the United States, as measured by goods and services produced, are the highest in the world.

★ ★ ★ ★ ★

Using PPPs, the United States had the highest per capita gross domestic product (GDP) in the world in 1990. The relative rankings for selected countries are presented in the chart below.

The obvious conclusion is that the living standards in the United States, as measured by goods and services produced, are the highest in the world.

PRODUCTIVITY

Contrary to what many people believe, the United States, overall, still has the most productive labor force in the world. According to a study by the McKinsey Global Institute, a research subsidiary of the internationally renowned consult-

PER CAPITA GDP USING PURCHASING POWER PARITIES
(Each country's value shown as a percent of U.S. GDP)

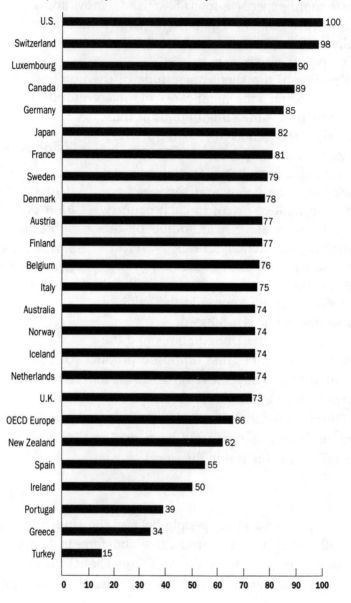

ing group, Japanese workers in 1990 were only 83 percent as productive as Americans, on average, weighting each industry by the number of workers it employed. German workers were only 79 percent as productive.[10] Japan did have higher productivity levels in steel, car parts, metalworking, car and consumer electronic industries. German labor productivity lags behind the U.S. in all categories except for steel and metalworking, where the levels of productivity are virtually identical to the U.S.

There is one troublesome aspect to the productivity story in the U.S., and that is that the growth in productivity has been slowing down as of late. From 1937 to 1989, productivity growth in the United States averaged 1.9 percent per year. But that average of 1.9 percent is made up of figures from two distinctly different periods. From 1937 to 1973, productivity increased at an average annual rate of 3 percent. Then from 1973 to 1989, productivity increased at a rate of only 0.9 percent per year.[11]

This is of some concern because increases in productivity are what make corresponding increases in the standard of living possible. A rate of 3 percent annual increase in productivity means a society will double its standard of living in just 23 years. At that rate, an individual could reasonably expect to see the standard of living more than triple over the span of his or her life. If, however, productivity is increasing by only 0.9 percent each year, it would take more than 77 years to double the living standards of society.

Productivity gains were steady from 1960 to 1973, then we seemed to hit a snag. Growth was slow from 1973 to 1982. Things picked up again in 1983, but we hit another snag in 1988. From 1988 to 1991, productivity gains were virtually nonexistent. Since 1991, however, we have started to see a return to increasing labor productivity.

7

AVERAGE ANNUAL GROWTH IN LABOR PRODUCTIVITY IN THE UNITED STATES

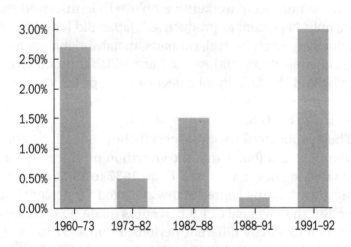

More concerns are often raised when the increases in U.S. productivity are compared with other countries. Looking at the average annual gains in productivity over the period from 1960 to 1986, we see that other countries' rates of growth in productivity are increasing faster than that of the United States.

How worried should we be about this slowdown in the growth of productivity? We should be somewhat concerned because, as we have seen, there is a connection between increases in productivity and increases in standards of living. However, the problem is not as significant as it may seem at first glance. Part of the problem stems from the way we go about measuring productivity. We look at the quantity of output generated relative to the quantity of input used in the process. This measure fails to take into account any improvements in quality of output. For example, a car that is poorly constructed and will last five years is given the same weight as a car that is extremely well built and will last twice as long. A cataract operation performed with a scalpel and needing stitches is counted the same as the identical procedure done with the benefit of laser technology. The invasiveness and recovery time of the two methods are drastically different, but the output is counted the same.

Ignoring quality improvements will significantly understate economic growth. Quality improvements are most difficult to measure in a service industry. For example, the advent of cash dispensing machines and a host of other new services in the financial industry go undetected by traditional measures of output. In transportation industries, output is measured by tonnage miles hauled. If a computer is introduced providing a driver with explicit directions for the shortest route to a given destination, miles hauled will decrease, giving the illusion of decreased productivity, when in reality, economic growth has occurred.[12]

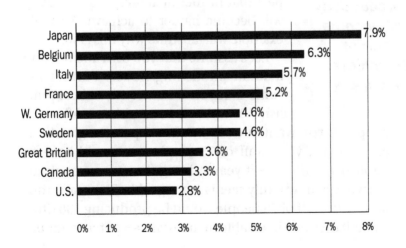

**AVERAGE YEARLY GAIN IN PRODUCTIVITY
1960–1986**

Japan	7.9%
Belgium	6.3%
Italy	5.7%
France	5.2%
W. Germany	4.6%
Sweden	4.6%
Great Britain	3.6%
Canada	3.3%
U.S.	2.8%

It is also important to recognize that the U.S. has been moving increasingly to a service-sector economy. From 1979 to 1989, employment in the service sector increased an average of 3.2 percent a year. In the goods-producing sector, employment fell by an annual 0.4 percent for that same period of time.

UCLA economist Michael Darby recalculated economic growth in the 1980s, taking into account the effects of understatement of services and other "noise" in the data due to rapidly decreasing prices in growth industries. He found that the officially recorded growth from 1979 to 1989 could have been understated by as much as a full percentage point and that growth in the 1980s was at least as strong as it was in the first eighty years of this century.[13]

To put the issue in perspective, remember that the U.S. already has a very high level of productivity, and it is logical to expect that further increases in productivity will become harder to achieve.

★ ★ ★ ★ ★

To put the issue in perspective, remember that the U.S. already has a very high level of productivity, and it is logical to expect that further increases in productivity will become harder to achieve. A simple example will illustrate why this is so.

Let's assume that you own and operate a small publishing house. Further assume that you are currently able to publish 100 titles a year with a staff of 75 people. If you wanted to maintain a 3 percent growth in productivity, your staff of 75 employees would have to publish 103 titles next year. Adding three more books to the workload certainly seems manageable. Ten years from now, your staff of 75 people would be producing 138 titles a year if they had been able to maintain a 3 percent annual increase in productivity. An additional 3 percent increase in year eleven would mean increasing production from 138 books to 142, a net increase of four instead of just three. After twenty years in business, your 75-member staff would be making 186 books a year. Increasing that number by 3 percent means 6 additional books in year 21. By now you're undoubtedly seeing that the size of the base makes a big difference in how much output must increase in absolute terms to maintain the same level of gains in relative productivity.

Now consider a ninety-year period. If you had started your business in 1900 with 75 employees producing 100 titles a year, by 1990 you would have to be producing 1,473 titles, still with 75 employees, to maintain an average 3 percent annual increase in productivity. Increasing output by 3 percent in 1900 meant adding 3 more titles. Increasing output by 3 percent in 1990 requires an additional 44 titles.

Furthermore, when a small publisher adds 3 titles to a current production level of 100, it represents a 3 percent increase. If a large publisher adds 15 titles to a current level of 1,000, it shows only a 1.5 percent increase in productivity. Adding five times as many titles in absolute terms shows up as only one-half of the relative gain in productivity.

The U.S. has the largest base level of productivity in the world. It has the largest level of economic output.

★ ★ ★ ★ ★

The same thing would be true for increases in living standards. If you currently are making $1,000 a year, a 3 percent increase in income means $1,030, or $30 more. If, however, your current income is $25,000, a one percent increase means $250 more in absolute terms. I ask you, would you rather have a $30 increase from $1,000 or a $250 increase from $25,000?

This is why growth-rate comparisons between countries are not all that relevant. Country-by-country comparisons become most useful when they are starting from relatively equal bases. The U.S. has the largest base level of productivity in the world. It has the largest level of economic output. Next to the United States, the second largest economy is Japan, which is about half as large in terms of gross national product. The economy of a country like South Korea would be less than 10 percent as large as the U.S. economy.

I do not mean to disparage other countries or to be unduly boastful about the United States simply because of the size of the relative economies. But the size of the existing level of economic output is important when you consider how much output must increase in absolute terms to sustain a trend of growth in productivity. Adding 3 percent to a 5 trillion dollar economy means increasing output by 150 billion dollars. That would roughly be the equivalent of adding the entire output of Taiwan to our existing economy just to achieve a 3 percent increase.

When considered in the context of the current size of the economy, productivity in the United States is something about which to be encouraged.

RESOURCES

Another of our great strengths lies in our endowment of resources. The geographic land mass of the United States consists of approximately one-sixteenth of the total land mass of the planet. That fraction more than doubles if you consider only land that is arable—that is, fit for the growing of crops. More than one-eighth of all the world's arable land lies within the borders of the United States. This allows Americans the luxury of living with relatively large amounts of space. The population density of the U.S. is only 70 people per square mile. The density in Japan is over eleven times as great, with 830 people per square mile. Germany and the United Kingdom are also relatively crowded, with population densities of 583 and 613 people per square mile, respectively.[14]

There is a great diversity of climate and geological composition throughout the fifty states, allowing Americans to enjoy not only a wide range of habitats within their geographical borders but also a great variety of animal life. A total of 1,090 different species of bird life and 466 species of mammals exist within the United States.[15]

Another of our great strengths lies in our endowment of resources.

★ ★ ★ ★ ★

The U.S. also has significant reserves of important minerals such as copper, lead, zinc, iron ore, molybdenum, tungsten, vanadium, titanium, and lithium.

The United States is the world's largest producer of energy. In 1991, a total of 67.35 quadrillion BTU's of energy was produced in the U.S., 32 percent of which came from coal, 27 percent from natural gas, and 23 percent from oil. By comparison for that same year, the former USSR produced 66.0 quadrillion BTU's; China, 30.19 quadrillion BTU's; Saudi Arabia, 19.98 quadrillion BTU's; Canada, 13.6 quadrillion BTU's; and the United Kingdom, 9.13 quadrillion BTU's.[16] Of the total world commercial energy produced in 1989, the U.S. produced 22.9 percent of the total energy derived from solids, 25.9 percent derived from liquids, 24.4 percent derived from gas, and 20.4 percent of the total production of electricity.[17] The production of electricity in the United States during the year 1991 was 3.4 times the amount produced in Japan, 4.8 times as much as was produced by Germany, and 8.9 times the quantity produced in the UK that same year. The gross nuclear energy produced by the U.S. represents about 30 percent of the world's total.[18] Our reserves of oil, natural gas, and coal amounted to approximately 2.5 percent, 3.8 percent, and 12 percent, respectively, of total known reserves in the world as of January 1991.[19]

CAPITAL STOCK

One of the principal reasons that we enjoy such a high level of productivity is the level of physical capital that we have: buildings, roads, bridges, and various types of industrial equipment. These all serve as an economic lever that multiplies the efforts of our labor force—another real benefit to our economy in general. One worker can produce a great deal more with proper equipment than would be possible if everything had to be handmade. The U.S. Department of Commerce estimated the gross stock of tangible wealth (equipment and structures) of the United States in 1991 to be $26.7 trillion (in 1991 dollars). That works out to be about $100,000 worth of physical assets per man, woman, and child in the United States.[20] A family of four could think of themselves as having close to $400,000 of physical capital (before depreciation) available to them in the economy. About 29 percent of the total physical assets consisted of residential assets. Private sector nonresidential structures, (factories, shopping malls, etc.) accounted for 19 percent. Roughly 18 percent consisted of equipment in the private sector. Only 6 percent was attributed to military equipment and structures. The total government-owned portion of physical assets amounted to about 18 percent. This would include the value of roads, bridges, public buildings, sewer-treatment systems, and other typical government assets.

TRANSPORTATION

We Americans like to get around. We travel for business; we travel for pleasure. Transportation brings us food, clothing, and most of the things we use in our lives each day. Transportation allows us to live in one place and work in another. It expands our horizons and brings the geographically diverse people of our nation together.

As a nation, we have a lot of cars in which to get around. In 1990, there were about 572 cars in use inside the U.S. for every 1,000 citizens. By comparison there were 297 cars per 1,000 people in Japan and 441 cars per 1,000 people in Germany. During the 1980s, Americans drove, on average, over 2.7 trillion miles per year. On a per capita basis, this would roughly translate into 10,800 miles per person each year.[21]

We take advantage of our extensive highway system through the use of commercial vehicles as well. There were over 45 million trucks on American highways in 1990, compared to 22.6 million in Japan and 2.7 million in Germany. That works out to be around one truck for every six people in the U.S. Throughout the 1980s, an average of 1.1 trillion metric tons of freight were shipped over our roads. That's about 4,500 metric tons per person.[22]

Almost 20 percent of all the railroad track in the world is laid on American soil. An average of 1.6 trillion metric tons per year were shipped on U.S. rails throughout the 1980s.[23] That works out close to 6,600 metric tons per person.

We also fly a lot. About 37 percent of all of the world's airports are in the United States.[24] In the 1980s, Americans averaged 693 billion miles of commercial aviation flight per year. The average American flew 2,700 miles per year throughout the 1980s. We also use the airways to move a great deal of freight. About 15 billion metric tons (on average) of freight were shipped by air each year throughout the United States during the 1980s.[25]

> **The United States is, without a doubt, a leader in the development of technology.**
>
> ★ ★ ★ ★ ★

The United States is blessed with an extensive inland-waterway system that can be used for shipping. U.S. inland waterways accounted for the shipment of close to 700 billion metric tons of freight each year throughout the 1980s.[26] That would be over thirteen times the amount shipped by inland waterways in France and eleven times the amount in the UK. The former USSR was second to the U.S. in this category, using its inland waterways system to ship 250 billion metric tons (about 36 percent of the tonnage shipped by the U.S.).

TECHNOLOGY

The United States is, without a doubt, a leader in the development of technology. One measure of its success is the number of patents awarded each year. In 1990, a total of 99,100 patents were issued by the U.S. patent office. The majority of those (53 percent) were issued to U.S. citizens and corporations. Japan claimed the next highest percentage with 21 percent, followed by Germany, which received about 8 percent of the awarded patents.

Americans have historically shown a real propensity for invention. As evidence of our bent to invent, consider the following list of just a few of the items that have been credited to U.S. inventors over the past two hundred years:[27]

1780 bifocal lens
1793 cotton gin
1804 screw propeller
1828 electromagnet
1834 reaper
1835 photographic paper
1837 magnetic telegraph
1839 vulcanized rubber
1845 rotary printing press
1846 sewing machine
1849 hydraulic turbine
1849 safety pin
1851 cylinder lock
1851 ice-making machine
1852 elevator brake
1860 shoe-sewing machine
1865 sleeping car
1865 web printing press
1867 railway block signals
1867 typewriter
1868 air brakes
1868 refrigerator car
1871 compressed air rock drill
1873 car coupler
1875 barbed wire
1876 carpet sweeper
1876 telephone
1877 microphone
1877 phonograph
1878 disc cultivator
1879 cash register
1882 electric fan
1884 electric trolley car
1884 fountain pen
1885 A.C. transformer
1885 adding machine
1887 record disc
1888 Kodak camera
1890 pneumatic hammer
1891 steel alloy
1891 submarine
1891 zipper
1892 color photography

1894 card time recorder
1894 movie machine
1895 bottle machine
1895 safety razor
1901 electric washer
1903 motorized airplane
1904 tractor crawler
1906 radio amplifier
1907 electric vacuum cleaner
1911 air-conditioning
1911 automobile self-starter
1911 hydro airplane
1912 airplane automatic pilot
1913 tungsten filament
1913 X-ray tube
1917 electric razor
1917 hybrid corn
1918 automatic toaster
1919 arc welder
1923 television
1924 frozen food
1925 circuit breaker
1928 radio beacon
1928 Teletype
1929 coaxial cable system
1933 FM 2 path radio
1935 Richter scale
1937 nylon
1938 fiberglass
1938 fluorescent lamp
1938 Teflon
1939 helicopter
1944 electron spectrometer
1945 Tupperware
1947 transistor
1948 Polaroid Land camera
1954 oral contraceptive
1959 integrated circuit
1960 minicomputer
1970 floppy disk
1972 compact disc
1982 artificial heart

RELATIVE SHARE OF GLOBAL MARKETS BY INDUSTRY (1990)

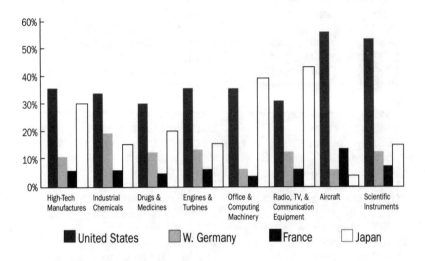

Another way to measure technological leadership is to analyze a country's relative share of the global technology market. This is done by the National Science Board (NSB) on a biannual basis. The NSB has provided the following estimates of market shares as of 1990.[28]

A review of the above data shows that the U.S. is still the world leader in terms of market share, with the exception of office and computing machinery and radio, TV, and communication equipment. All countries have lost market share to the Japanese over the last decade. However, this is not necessarily the disaster it is often painted to be. The size of the entire world market has grown. As other countries develop their economies, the U.S. can expect its share of all world markets to decline. That is what global economic development is all about. Japan has enjoyed a disproportionate share of this new growth, but it does not

**CONTRIBUTION OF SELECTED COUNTRIES
TO WORLD LITERATURE (1987)**

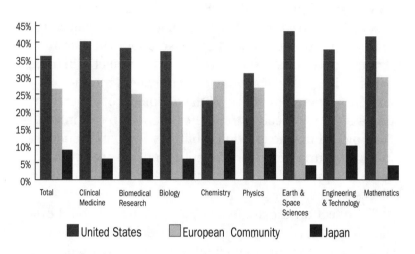

necessarily mean that all other countries are worse off in absolute terms. Furthermore, this new competition provides motivation for other countries to do better in terms of production efficiency and quality improvement.

Technological development can also be assessed by examining what is happening in our universities regarding research and development. Successful scholarly research activity is often judged by publication in academic journals. Before an article is accepted for publication, it must undergo rigid review by other experts in the field. The chart above shows that U.S. institutions are still a dominant force in the scholarship of technological disciplines.[29] The U.S. percentage of total contributions to scholarly literature in 1987 was 35.6 percent. It had remained virtually unchanged since 1981, when it accounted for 35.9 percent.

Money and Financial Capital

While presenting a seminar on money, banking, and finance issues to a group of Soviet officials and business executives who were visiting the United States, I decided to dramatize a point I wished to make about the nature of money. I asked one of the participants for a sheet of his note paper. I then asked if anyone else could lend me a ten-dollar bill for a moment or two. With both pieces of paper in my possession, I proceeded to rip the notebook paper in two. I then picked up the ten-dollar bill. My Russian friend was looking a little worried. His apprehension was well deserved: I proceeded to tear his ten-dollar bill into two pieces as well.

The effect on the audience was more than I could ever have hoped for. My translator was speechless. The participants, in perfect unison, all let out a gasp that would be difficult to orchestrate under any other circumstance. The Russian donor looked positively pale.

I feigned total surprise at their reaction, claiming I could not understand their dismay. After all, it was just a piece of paper. They didn't react that way when I tore up the notebook paper. "What was the difference?" I asked.

This is always a most amazing discussion, no matter what the circumstances are under which it takes place. What is so magical about a piece of paper we call a ten-dollar bill, a five-dollar bill, or any other denomination for that matter? What stands behind it?

Absolutely nothing!

That's right. There is no gold, no silver, no diamonds, nor any promises of the United States government to back the dollar. Our currency is simply paper that is printed by the Bureau of Engraving and Printing and issued by the Federal Reserve Banking System.

Then why should anyone be alarmed when their ten-dollar bill gets torn in two? The reason is that a ten-dollar bill is money. Money is a store of value, and when you lose a ten-dollar bill, you lose the equivalent of ten dollars' worth of purchasing power or ten dollars' worth of value. Even though there is nothing that specifically backs our currency, it works well as a store of value.

People believe in the dollar in a big way. Currency issued during World War II still circulates today as far away as the remote jungles of Cambodia. It is worn, faded, and tattered, but it still serves its purpose as a medium of exchange and as a store of value. In fact, most of the United States currency today circulates outside of the U.S. In 1974, according to a Federal Reserve survey, only 15 percent of all U.S. currency was held for transaction purposes by domestic residents.[30] The Federal Reserve estimates that two-thirds of all new currency that is printed winds up being used outside of the United States.[31]

The universal acceptance of the dollar is probably the most tangible piece of evidence that we have to demonstrate the underlying strength of the United States economy relative to the rest of the world.

★ ★ ★ ★ ★

The universal acceptance of the dollar is probably the most tangible piece of evidence that we have to demonstrate the underlying strength of the United States economy relative to the rest of the world. Dollars are ultimately only as strong as the economy that backs them; and that is the only thing backing them.

What about inflation, you say? Doesn't inflation erode the value of a dollar?

Inflation is generally perceived as being a bad thing, and rightly so. But inflation doesn't necessarily mean that all forms of money denominated in dollars will lose value. The purchasing power of money that is held in the form of coin and currency will indeed be eroded by inflation. But most Americans have traditionally held their money balances in interest-bearing accounts. The nominal interest rates paid on such balances normally compensate depositors in such a way that the real purchasing power of their money is not being eroded. In our worst years of inflation, from 1973 to 1981, only about 19 percent of liquid assets was held in a non-interest-bearing form such as currency or non-interest-bearing checking accounts.[32]

Inflation rates in the United States have also been historically low when compared to other countries around the world. The average annual compound rate of inflation in the United States from 1930 to 1992 was 3.74 percent.[33] Peru's rate of inflation in 1989 was over 7,400 percent. That same year Brazil experienced 2,938 percent inflation. Israel averaged 118.5 percent annual increases in consumer prices from 1980 to 1989.[34]

Not only are dollars a good form of money, but the financial system of the United States also makes dollars relatively easy to acquire and use as financial capital for building businesses, making investments in government infrastructure, and financing consumer purchases such as housing, automobiles, and appliances.

In 1992, state and local governments were able to raise $22 billion to finance projects in education, $17 billion for transportation projects, $20 billion for conservation and utilities, $22 billion for social welfare, $5 billion for industrial aid, and another $30 billion for other purposes. All told, state and local governments were able to raise $215 billion in 1992, 44 percent of which went to refinance existing debt with the remaining 56 percent being used for new projects.[35]

What happens to all of these dollars? They don't merely hibernate away as inert pieces of paper or sit idle as silent numbers on a dusty bank ledger. Our financial system converts dollars into value-creating factories, roads, bridges, schools, farm equipment, computers, and such. This type of investment is an important topic, and one that we will address more completely in chapter 3.

U.S. corporations also benefited significantly from the capital markets, raising $559 billion of long-term financial capital in 1992. Most of that amount (84 percent, or $471 billion) came from the bond markets. Just as it was with state and local governments, the majority of these bonds (73 percent, or $345 billion) were used to refinance existing debt and take advantage of lower interest rates. New issues of corporate stock accounted for the remaining 16 percent ($88 billion) of long-term financial capital raised by corporations in 1992.[36] This money was used to finance new buildings, new factories, increased inventories, investments in equipment, and other things that help the economy grow, creating jobs and increasing output.

New housing construction was financed by $123 million in new home mortgages in 1993. As of the third quarter of 1993, mortgages outstanding on family residences amounted to $3.4 trillion dollars. This represents a huge investment by Americans in other Americans. The extensive and active mortgage market is one of the key ingredients in our economy that allows so many citizens to enjoy the high standard of housing that we have.

> *The extensive and active mortgage market is one of the key ingredients in our economy that allows so many citizens to enjoy the high standard of housing that we have.*
>
> ★ ★ ★ ★ ★

ECONOMIC OPPORTUNITY

What do you suppose would happen if the United States suddenly opened its borders and allowed unrestricted immigration to anyone who would choose to live here? No doubt there would be a flood of people coming with the hope of bettering their lives. The United States, ever since its colonial days, has been considered a land of opportunity.

One of the first reasons to come to the United States is because that is where the jobs have been. A good way of judging economic opportunity is to see how many jobs are being created. The ability to absorb workers in the marketplace and to use them productively in value-creating endeavors is key to the long-term success of any economy. Civilian employment (ages sixteen and over) in 1947 numbered just over 57 million people. By 1992, that number had grown to over 117 million. That represents an average increase of 1.6 percent per year. That may not sound like much, but it has outpaced the rate of increase in population to the extent that civilian labor force participation rates have steadily increased from 58.8 percent of the population in 1948 to 66.3 percent in 1992. Furthermore, while the number of jobs in the U.S. has nearly doubled since 1960, employment in the European Community has increased by only 10 percent during that same period. For comparison, labor force participation rates for other selected countries are presented in the chart on page 25.

The other side of the picture is unemployment. Being unemployed is certainly an economic hardship. From 1980 to 1992, unemployment in the U.S. averaged 7.0 percent, while fluctuating between a low of 5.2 percent in 1989 and a high of 9.5 percent in 1982. The hardship of unemployment is not shared equally among developed countries. In the European Community, unemployment over the last de-

24

**LABOR FORCE PARTICIPATION RATES
SELECTED COUNTRIES (1991)**

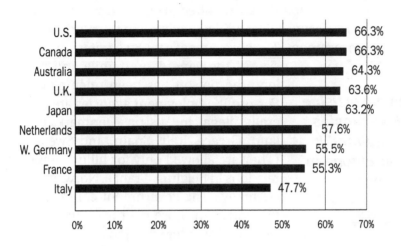

cade (1984–1993) has averaged 10 percent and never once dipped below 8 percent. In October 1993, the EC was suffering over 12 percent unemployment, a full five percentage points higher than the 7 percent unemployment in the United States at that same time. The duration of unemployment in Europe is also much longer. Almost half of Europe's unemployed have been that way for more than a year. In America, the equivalent figure is only 11 percent.[37]

Such dramatically different statistics raise the question of what structural differences exist, between the labor climates of Europe and the United States, that may explain such differences in unemployment. David Henderson has spent some time comparing the U.S. and European labor markets and has concluded that the labor markets in Europe are overregulated and inflexible when compared to the United States.[38]

Hiring workers in Europe is at best a difficult and un-

25

pleasant task for an employer who is concerned about productivity and the quality of his or her workers. In Italy, for example, companies are required to rank and subsequently hire prospective job candidates according to criteria set by the government. The government's top two criteria are the size of the candidate's family and how long the person has been unemployed. For-profit employment agencies are generally illegal in Austria, Denmark, Finland, Greece, Italy, Spain, and Sweden. (They are allowed only for filling temporary jobs in Belgium, France, Norway, and Germany.) The government controls job placement in those countries, including who gets hired for what jobs.

> **Even advertising job vacancies is regulated in some European countries.**
>
> ★ ★ ★ ★ ★

Even advertising job vacancies is regulated in some European countries. Belgium, France, and Sweden require companies to notify the government of any job for which they plan to recruit from outside the firm. According to the Organization for Economic Cooperation and Development (OECD), it appears, in Spain, "to be illegal to advertise a job at all until a contract of employment for it has been submitted to, and approved by, the placement service." [39]

If it is difficult to hire workers in Europe, it is even harder to terminate employment. To dismiss a worker in Germany, an employer must give the person two to three months' notice. In addition, the government Works Council must be consulted on the case and can then override the dismissal if it is deemed that it is "socially unwarranted." Any appeals would go to labor court. Throughout this period of time, the employee must be retained on the payroll.

In Italy, employers are required to supply proof to support that any dismissal is just. France allows dismissal for gross misconduct but, if the termination is deemed to have been for financial reasons, the dismissed employee can claim compensation. Portugal also allows dismissal for gross misconduct but does not recognize incompetence as a legitimate cause for termination.

Because temporary workers could easily be used to circumvent these laws, European governments have greatly restricted the ability of firms to use temporary workers. Italy and Sweden do not allow private temporary work agencies. Germany bans the use of temporary workers in the construction industry and limits employment of temporary workers in other industries to a maximum of five months.

European nations generally provide richer packages of unemployment benefits than the U.S. does, which can discourage people from finding new jobs. Loss of health-care benefits is not an issue because health care is provided by the government. In the Netherlands, unemployment compensation for a single forty-year-old worker would amount to 70 percent of previous earnings. In France and Germany it would be close to 60 percent of previous earnings. These benefits can run as long as two and a half years in France, three years in the Netherlands, and one year in Germany. In the United States, unemployment benefits run at about 50 percent of previous compensation, exclude health care, and have traditionally expired after six months. Is it any wonder that 90 percent of unemployed U.S. workers find a job in less than six months while almost half of all unemployed Europeans have been collecting unemployment benefits for more than a year?

> *Employment opportunity is a good reason to live in the United States. There is also opportunity to dramatically improve your income.*
>
> ★ ★ ★ ★ ★

The bottom line is that 77 percent of Americans of working age have jobs while only 67 percent of Europeans of working age are, in fact, working. Roughly one out of every four persons under the age of twenty-five in France cannot find employment. That's twice the comparable rate in the United States. Even Sweden, which has long been considered the model country for its social maintenance of employment, is now experiencing a 10 percent unemployment rate.

In the past century, we have moved steadily away from an agricultural society toward a more service-oriented society. In the year 1900, almost 12 million people, 40.2 percent of the American labor force, were engaged in agriculture. Ninety years later, only 2.7 percent of the labor force (3.3 million people) was engaged in agricultural types of employment. And they had to feed a much larger country and a greater portion of the world. Why did that happen? It happened because we became very good at farming and increased our levels of productivity to the point where we did not need all of those people working on farms.

Is this a bad thing? It means that very few of us now live or work on farms. It means there are a lot fewer opportunities for a career in agriculture. But there are new opportunities today that people living in 1900 could not even have imagined.

Occupational Employment Statistics project job growth from 1990 to the year 2005 to exceed 50 percent for home-health aides, personal and home-care aides, medical secretaries, systems analysts, computer programmers and scientists, medical assistants, travel agents, management analysts, flight attendants, and child care-workers.[40]

New employment opportunities are also created by new and growing businesses. The total number of business concerns in the U.S. has increased by an average of 9.3 percent per year from 1980 to 1992. In 1980 there were 2.78 million businesses. By 1992, just twelve years later, that number had soared to over 8.8 million businesses. Innovation that comes with large numbers of new small employers is very important because that is where most private employment occurs. As can be seen below, over 55 percent of nongovernment employees in the United States work for a firm with less than 100 employees.

PRIVATE SECTOR EMPLOYMENT BY SIZE CATEGORY (1990)

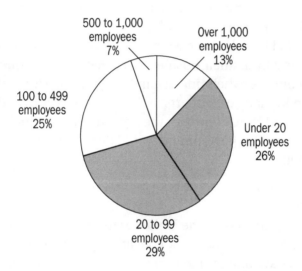

In addition to this, there were 10 million self-employed Americans in 1992, up from 8.6 million in 1980.

Employment opportunity is a good reason to live in the United States. There is also opportunity to dramatically improve your income. This happens on a regular basis. The University of Michigan conducted a study on income mobility and found that large segments of people in the U.S. do, in fact, significantly improve their relative income levels over time. Of those families ranking in the lowest fifth by income in 1980, 35 percent were able to move out of the lowest fifth within four years. More than 5 percent of the lowest-income families in 1980 moved into the highest 40 percent by 1984.[41]

These facts demonstrate that the opportunities to either take a job or to make a job in the United States are relatively good, and that millions of Americans are indeed taking advantage of these opportunities. It also demonstrates the dangers of trying to become more like Europe in the way we regulate our business activities, especially for small businesses.

As a CPA, I have had occasion to work with people trying to start or run a small business. The regulatory requirements seem overwhelming. Even though it is easier in the U.S. than in many other parts of the world, it is still harder than it should be to cope with the ever-increasing amounts of regulation. Our government would do well not to add to the burden.

EDUCATION

Another opportunity in the United States that is closely related to economic welfare is education. Even though our educational systems are far from perfect, educational opportunities for the average citizen are abundant by world standards. Our commitment to education is clear. Measuring by purchasing power parities, the U.S. in 1988 spent 42 percent more on educating a primary or secondary student than Japan did, and 61 percent more than West Germany.[42]

Our commitment to education extends all the way through the college or university level. Again in 1988, 13 percent of Japan's population had completed university or college levels of education. In West Germany, the percentage was even lower: 10 percent. The U.S. by contrast had 23 percent of its population completing college or university. At the university level, the U.S. outspent Japan on a per-student basis by 61 percent and West Germany by almost 100 percent.[43]

As Europe tries to come to grips with its high rates of chronic unemployment, new levels of global competition, and the increasing pace of technological change, Europeans are beginning to rethink the way they do job training and education. As noted in *The Economist*,

> Surprisingly, the training system which seems to be coping best with technological innovation and global competition is the most maligned of the lot, the American one. . . . Indeed, the American tradition of providing people with masses of general academic education, including a start at university for half the population and plenty of second chances for everyone, and leaving specific training to the market, is becoming more, rather than less relevant. Economists have long argued that the returns on general education are higher than those on specific training, because education is transferable whereas many skills tend to be job-specific.[44]

Education in the United States is a basic strength and not a weakness. To invest in the education of a society is to invest in the economic future of that society. Our past investments have paid off. Now we need to maintain past educational standards, and we must embrace the opportunity to improve as well.

National Balance Sheet

Debt is a literal four-letter word that is often treated as a "four- letter word." It really shouldn't be. Debt is most often the flip side of investment, which people generally perceive as being something good. The capital markets serve the purpose of translating savings into investment. People buy stocks and bonds, make deposits in savings accounts and certificates of deposits, and make payments to life insurance companies for policies that provide them with retirement benefits. These various flows of funds into a variety of financial institutions find their way back into the economy in the form of economic assets.

There is a great deal of concern about the magnitude of debt outstanding in the United States. One way to try to put debt into perspective is to relate it to the value of assets that are financed by that debt, much the same way we analyze the burden of a mortgage on our home. When you do this for the United States, it becomes apparent that the picture is not all that bad.

At the end of 1992, the net value of all tangible structures and equipment in both the private and government sectors approached $16 trillion dollars.[45] The total credit market debt owed by the domestic nonfinancial sector of the United States at the end of 1992 amounted to $11.7 trillion. Of this total, 26 percent represented federal government debt, 8 percent represented state and local government debt, with the remaining 65 percent representing obligations of households and businesses.

This means that the nation is carrying a mortgage roughly equal to 73 percent of the value of its assets. Another way of thinking about it is that equity in these assets amounts to about 27 percent. Bear in mind that the only assets that I have included are the tangible assets of structures and equipment. Endowments of natural resources and intangible assets like the educational investment in our people, the value of patents, and our economic know-how are all important economic resources that have not been included.

Relating the size of the federal debt to the size of the economy is also useful, in the same way that comparing a mortgage to your annual income is useful for getting a handle on the measure of the burden of debt. The federal debt as a percentage of the total value of domestically produced goods and services in 1993 was about 69 percent. The estimates for 1995 place it at about 71 percent of GDP. Historically that percentage has been as high as 127.5 percent in 1946, when the U.S. had to finance its war effort in World War II.

Even though the absolute size of the amount of federal government debt is overwhelming, when it is compared to the even larger size of the economy as a whole, it becomes apparent that it is manageable.

★ ★ ★ ★ ★

Putting it in more personal terms, having a debt-to-GDP percentage of 71 percent would mean that if you had an income of $30,000 a year, your mortgage would be about $21,000. That doesn't sound nearly as ominous as saying that the national debt is over $4.5 trillion, but it is probably more useful in trying to ascertain how much of a burden the debt actually puts on the economy.

Please understand that I am not trying to encourage or even justify more government spending. It is not healthy, in the long run, for a government to continually spend more than it can reasonably and legitimately collect in taxes. Neither is it healthy to have the federal government's share of economic activity increasing. These things are problems.

Nor am I attempting to justify government's past expenditures that have resulted in the national debt we have today. What I do want to do is try to give some perspective on the issue so we can make reasonable judgments as to the magnitude of the problems of the U.S. economy.

Given the data, even though the absolute size of the amount of federal government debt is overwhelming, when it is compared to the even larger size of the economy as a whole, it becomes apparent that it is manageable. I believe we need to work hard at changing the direction we are going, but meanwhile the economy will not be crushed under the weight of the national debt.

A very important question related to all of this is, How difficult is it to service this debt? In 1992, the federal government paid about $220 billion dollars in interest. But since 15 percent of that was paid to itself, net interest paid amounted to only $187 billion. Most of it (81 percent) was paid to individuals and businesses in the U.S., and 19 percent ($41.2 billion) went to the rest of the world.[46]

On a personal level, I understand that when I pay interest I am becoming poorer. But when a government pays interest, it isn't at all clear that the nation is poorer. It depends on who gets the interest. In the case of the United States, the vast majority of interest is paid to its own citizens, who, by the way, pay taxes to the government so the government can give it back as interest. Most of the taxes paid in the United States are collected from the people with the highest incomes: The upper 40 percent of Americans by income level pay over 81 percent of the income taxes. This is virtually the same group of people who have lent money to the government, when they have purchased U.S. treasury bonds and notes. The interest they collect on these investments comes from the taxes they pay. This financial exchange does not necessarily make the nation any poorer. The only real cost is the loss in economic efficiency resulting from this circular flow of money that could be put to better use.

Paying interest to our own citizens doesn't sound as bad as paying interest to foreigners. But allow me to try to put this into perspective as well. It's interesting to note that in 1992 Americans spent nearly twice as much on alcoholic beverages as we paid to foreigners in interest on the federal debt.

If you add up what Americans spent in 1992 on jewelry and watches ($34 billion), barbershops and beauty care ($24 billion), tobacco products ($51 billion), and alcoholic beverages ($77 billion), it would be just about the same as the net interest paid by the federal government to service the national debt.

Interest paid by the federal government is a significant portion of its annual expenditures, amounting to nearly 15 percent in 1992. But as a fraction of the total economy, it is a much less ominous number. Net interest on the federal debt in 1992 amounted to about 3 percent of the total value of goods and services produced domestically in the United States that year.[47] Foreign interest paid would amount to only 0.7 percent of gross domestic product.

When it comes to interest for state and local governments, they turn out to be big winners in the interest game. In 1992, state and local governments paid $66.1 billion in interest but received $112.1 billion of interest in return, netting them $46 billion in revenues.

Consumers are in much the same category as state and local governments. In 1992 consumers received $694.3 billion in interest and paid $111.1 billion. That means that for every $1 paid in interest by consumers in 1992, they received $6.25 in interest from investments.[48]

The business sector of our economy, from mom-and-pop delis to General Motors, pays the most interest on an annual basis. In 1992, a total of $442 billion in interest was paid by domestic industry, roughly double what was spent by the federal government that same year.[49]

In conclusion, our balance sheet is not nearly as bad as some would paint it. It could be and should be stronger, but by every reasonable standard, the nation is on solid financial footing.

POLITICAL AND LEGAL STABILITY

People often think about our legal system in much the same way they think about rush hour traffic. The usual connotations to rush hour are traffic jams, frustration, waiting, tensions, and gridlock. Yet an honest appraisal should force one to conclude that the rush hour phenomenon is more remarkable for its successes than its failures. Every day, millions of people leave their homes at approximately the same time and reach a specific destination with a remarkable degree of regularity and efficiency.

The same can be said of our legal system. Every day properties are bought and sold with a great deal of certainty about the transfer of legal rights. Short-term and long-term contracts are established and executed with confidence. A wide range of financial instruments are negotiated without anyone giving a thought to the possible legal ambiguities associated with the financial instrument itself. Businesses are formed and operate with an understanding of the rights, privileges, and corresponding responsibilities that go with operating an enterprise. Taxes are collected and paid with regularity. Estates are planned and can be executed in strict accordance with the desires of the decedent for generations to come. Real injuries and damages can be redressed by the poorest and most common of citizens.

But it is the failures of our legal system that capture our attention. The abuses, the delays, the errors in judgment, and the corruption are what get reported in the media because, by definition, it is the exception to the rule that makes news. To appreciate our legal system, all you need to do is talk to someone who has recently tried to draw up a contract in the former Soviet Union or attempted to start a joint venture in Ukraine or tried to buy a building in Romania. Their stories will help you begin to understand the comparative strength of our legal system.

The investment that our society has made in its legal framework makes it possible to plan for the future. Long-term economic growth requires long-term investment. That can only happen when there is a stable and mature legal system that defines and protects the personal, political, and economic rights of the citizenry. Long-term capital flows to those economies where there is long-term security.

The legal system of the United States has a history longer than the two-hundred-plus years of the nation's history. Our legal system can look back even beyond the ancient Roman law for its roots and is today an extension in the evolution of English common law. When faced with new legal challenges brought on by technological advances and changing economic structures, there is no legal vacuum but rather a rich historical and philosophical framework from which new problems can be addressed.

A void in the historical and philosophical legal framework can be a real problem for developing countries or emerging republics where, for the last generation or more, the Communist Party has been the only law, and before that, a czar or some other absolute monarch exercised authoritarian rule. Without the Communist Party, without the monarch, there is no system of law.

Closely linked to the system of law is the system of governance. Economic development is difficult, if not impossible, in the absence of a stable political situation. Consider the current plight of Africa. Nineteen countries in Africa are poorer today than they were twenty-five years ago. One in every two Africans has lost ground over this time compared with only one in twenty Asians and one in four Latin Americans. Children in Africa today are more likely to have their development stunted by lower birth weight, higher malnutrition, and poorer access to primary education than African children born in the late 1970s or early 1980s.[50]

> **Economic development is difficult, if not impossible, in the absence of a stable political situation.**
>
> ★ ★ ★ ★ ★

In searching for answers to why this has happened, Lawrence Summers of the World Bank points to at least

> one simple but often neglected lesson. War stops development. Almost all of the 36 countries that have lost ground over the last 25 years have been involved in a substantial military conflict. The Middle East is often thought of as the world's tinderbox; yet relative to population, Africans have three times as high a war fatality rate. In the last 30 years, wars have claimed nearly seven million victims, either directly or indirectly, by making the provision of food and basic social services difficult or impossible.[51]

When people cannot solve their differences by a political or legal process, they turn to war. We sometimes say that political campaigns are distasteful and can even get ugly. However, even our dirtiest politics are pristine when compared to the alternative of war.

Every four years in the United States, something remarkable happens. The powers of state and governance are passed peacefully from one set of hands to another. New leadership and new directions emerge by the consent of the people. The leader and direction may not have been the first choice of all citizens, but all citizens do stand in common agreement, supporting the basic process.

The government of the United States has been criticized for its largesse and seemingly insufferably slow response in addressing the nation's problems. Indeed, no one would advocate a system of governance that was unresponsive to the needs and concerns of its citizens. But stability in government is something that is to be valued in that it is necessary for long-term economic development. Stability and adaptability are two qualities that a government needs to be able to balance. If there is a fault with our current political system, it may be that it is *too* stable. And yet we ought not let our national impatience diminish our appreciation of stability in governance. Without it, there can be little hope of economic growth.

MARKET ECONOMY FRAMEWORK

There remains one more important strength that needs to be addressed, and to which we will now turn. The United States economy is predominantly a market economy. Market economies have a philosophical and theoretical framework that nurtures a society adept at creating economic value. Just how important is a philosophical and theoretical framework to a strong economy?

Can you recall the last time you visited the downtown section of a large city? Do you remember looking at those skyscrapers? You can always spot the folks who don't spend much time in the city: They're the ones with necks craning upward, watching the buildings vault to the heavens above. It is with a true sense of wonder that one considers these architectural and engineering feats. Yet I sincerely doubt that many people ever make the effort, at moments such as these, to turn their thoughts downward and contemplate the depths to which the foundation for such a monument must reach.

It is certain that the engineers and architects made no such oversight. They understood the importance of a solid and true foundation. The greater the building, the more important the foundation. To construct a great tower on a faulty foundation would jeopardize the lives and well-being of many in the future who were to depend on this building.

So it is with the first principles of economic systems. The systems will be as sound as the principles upon which they are based. First principles are so important and yet so often overlooked. People will get caught up with only those parts that are visible and essentially ignore the support structure lying below the surface. A proper inspection of any building should begin with its foundation, and the same is true of economics.

It is impossible for Christians to consider a framework for anything—including the framework of our economic system—without asking, Where does God fit in? A Christian should legitimately analyze God's role in the economic order—or rather, the capacity of the social economy to align itself in accordance with God's revealed desires and laws.

In the next several chapters, we will examine various strengths inherent in a market economy such as ours. Elements to be examined include the role of credit, private property, the profit motive, economic competition, and government. As we examine these different components of a market economy, we will also consider how they are compatible with—and how they diverge from—Christian principles. Then, in chapter 7, we will shift our focus to personal finances: how a proper understanding of our market economy, together with biblical principles, should affect the way we handle our money as individuals. In the final chapter, we will look briefly at the defining question of economics: how value is determined.

The U.S. economy is not a terminal case. We have a tremendous economic foundation on which to build for the future.

★ ★ ★ ★ ★

The United States is not a perfect society, nor is our economic system a perfect one. We have a tremendous amount of work ahead of us to solve our problems. But given our basic strengths, I am convinced that the U.S. economy is not a terminal case. We have a tremendous economic foundation on which to build for the future.

CHAPTER 2

Lending for Spending—
It Just Might Be the Neighborly
Thing to Do

Credit

I CAN'T REMEMBER exactly what he wanted. I *can* remember that it cost around fifty dollars. (Funny how the mind works sometimes.) I remember the cost because my son had calculated out just how many weeks' allowance he would have to forgo if I advanced him the cash to buy whatever it was he wanted. He was, in effect, wanting to borrow against what he felt confident was a steady stream of future income. Without my ever having to teach him, my son had figured out credit.

What to do? I took some time to deeply consider the matter (about half a second) and then gave him my reply.

"NO!"

Now you may consider my actions in this matter to be somewhat rash. After all, what difference would there be if he got his allowance all in one shot instead of in smaller, incremental amounts? In terms of the absolute amount of money he would receive, there would have been no difference. But in terms of learning how to save, live within a budget, and come to grips with some of the financial realities of life, there was a tremendous difference. I am a former banker. I am familiar with the dangers of debt, and I wasn't anxious to reinforce my son's acquisitive behavior.

When it comes to debt, I want my son to remember the example of Jake Houston. Jake was a cowboy. He was a real cowboy—not just a city-slicker wanna-be. His entire livelihood came from raising horses and cattle out in the vast grasslands of eastern Montana.

Jake was driving a herd of horses across the open range and, as will happen, one of the horses cut away from the herd and needed to be chased down. With one swift movement, Jake grabbed his rope and heel-kicked his horse into a full gallop in pursuit of the stray.

The sea of grass and the flat horizons of eastern Montana belie the irregularity of the terrain. In addition to the isolated buttes that stick out like warts on the landscape, there are deep and sudden ravines. The land is also pitted with prairie-dog holes. It was one of these that caused Jake's horse to stumble, hurling both horse and rider to the ground.

The fall came at the height of the chase when horse and cowboy were most vulnerable. Jake had been standing tall with his legs locked stiff and straight in his stirrups, ready to fling his lasso around the neck of the runaway. Then came the fall.

The angle and force of the fall broke the neck of Jake's horse, and it died instantly. Jake was alive and in one piece, but he found himself trapped under his dead horse. He tried for hours to dig out enough space from under the dead animal to pull himself free. But hard rock lies below the thin Montana topsoil, and he was unsuccessful.

Jake was able to reach his rope, and he realized that if he could just rope a nearby sagebrush, he might be able to pull the horse away with the aid of a Spanish windlass—a way of using a looped rope to create torque by twisting it with the aid of a lever. In this case, the lever was a branch from a sagebrush. Although the Spanish windlass has served many a cowboy in his day, it failed to serve Jake. He remained trapped.

Maybe time would come to his rescue. But this was eastern Montana, where a man could ride for days and meet only his shadow. As a last resort, Jack pulled out his jackknife. He propped himself up on one elbow and proceeded to eviscerate the horse as best he could. If only he could lighten the load, maybe he could finally extricate himself. It was a desperate measure, but it, too, failed.

The story was reported in a local small-town newspaper of eastern Montana around 1920, after Jake's body had been found. The facts were all there, preserved in the dust of the ground and retold by the sagebrush, the winch, the horse, and the knife.

What is the lesson of Jake Houston? Do we learn from this story that cowboys should not ride horses? Of course not. The horse is a tremendous help to the cowboy. It is hard to imagine that his work could be accomplished without the aid of his horse. However, as useful as horses are, they are not always safe. Credit is like that horse. It has a legitimate, even necessary role, but there are dangers associated with its use. People and organizations can find themselves trapped under its dead weight, having to resort to desperate measures to extricate themselves.

Credit certainly is a pervasive element of the modern market economy. And if there is one element in the market economy that has caused more confusion in the minds of Christians than anything else, it is the issue of credit.

LENDING FOR INVESTMENT—A NEIGHBORLY THING TO DO

Credit is the flip side of investment. It is an enabling force in a modern economy that increases the welfare of society as a whole. While it can and has been grossly misused, credit at its best is entirely compatible with such traditional Judeo-Christian values as honesty, commitment to your promises, stewardship of resources, and the Golden Rule. Credit enables us to store the value we create in such a way that the value is not only preserved but can be used to create even more value in the future.

This can be illustrated by a simple example. Let's say that for some reason, you decided to store your value in the form of a tool that extracts weeds. (We'll call it a weeder.) You have a weeder but you don't have a garden. Your neighbor, on the other hand, has a garden plot but doesn't have a weeder. It is reasonable to believe that if you lent your weeder to your neighbor, that garden would be significantly more productive. It also only seems fair that your neighbor should share some of the increased produce with you since it was, after all, your tool that helped grow more produce. The end result is that both you and your neighbor are better off. That neighbor was in a position to make good use of the value you originally created but didn't have an immediate use for.

In this example, you had a neighbor who could use your weeder—a very specialized situation. The clever thing about money is that it is unlimited in its usefulness for transfering value from one person to another. Money can always be converted into just what is needed to create even more value. *Interest* is simply the sharing of the additional output that is created. Paying interest is no different from the neighbor sharing some of the extra garden produce that was generated from the use of the weeding tool. Lending and paying interest on a loan become the neighborly things to do.

To withhold that tool from your neighbor would not seem like a nice thing to do. And for your neighbor to refuse to share any of the extra vegetables that the weeder helped grow would also seem unfair. Doing unto your neighbor as you would have him do unto you, in this case, means lending the tool and sharing the output. The fact that we have the modern financial convenience of money doesn't change the qualitative issues of credit. Storing your value as money in a mattress is equivalent to not letting your neighbor use your weeder.

LENDING FOR SPENDING—A DIFFERENT STORY

Credit, so far, seems easily justified by appealing to neighborliness. But the discussion has really focused on loans that are of a productive nature. There are other types of loans, such as those made for purposes of consumption. In the case of consumption loans, value is neither preserved nor increased but, rather, consumed. In the case where an individual has created value in excess of his ability or desire to consume, then that value can be transferred (lent) to someone else for the borrower's own consumption. If the value that was lent is to be repaid, it must come from any value that the borrower will create in the future. In this situation, there is no increase to share and the role of interest is not as clear.

Admonitions in Scripture that deal with credit relate to this type of a loan. In the agrarian, theocratic society of the Hebrews, wealth was held in the form of land and livestock. Certainly gold, silver, and precious stones were known and served as a store of value, but it was predominantly a barter economy, where money played only a minor role in the daily economic affairs of the people. If you wanted to talk wealth, you talked land, sheep, goats, and camels.

If you did lend, it was most likely for someone else's consumption. This would mean that the borrower's needs for consumption exceeded his ability to create or provide enough value to meet them. Scripture encourages lending in these situations.

> Good will come to him who is generous and lends freely, who conducts his affairs with justice. (Psalm 112:5)

But to lend in this situation and expect return payment in excess of what was originally given was considered wrong. It would even seem wrong in our culture today. It would be like lending a cup of sugar to a neighbor and expecting to receive more than a cup in return. We normally expect our neighbor to return only the amount borrowed. To expect anything more in return would be taking unfair advantage of someone else's need. It is in this light that biblical teachings on interest, such as the following, can be understood:

> Do not charge your brother interest, whether on money or food or anything else that may earn interest. You may charge a foreigner interest, but not a brother Israelite, so that the Lord your God may bless you in everything you put your hand to in the land you are entering to possess. (Deuteronomy 23:19-20)

In cases when the need is great, there is merit in treating a consumption loan as an outright gift, not expecting *anything* in return.

Give to the one who asks you, and do not turn away from the one who wants to borrow from you. (Matthew 5:42)

And if you lend to those from whom you expect repayment, what credit is that to you? Even "sinners" lend to "sinners," expecting to be repaid in full. But love your enemies, do good to them, and lend to them without expecting to get anything back. Then your reward will be great, and you will be sons of the Most High, because he is kind to the ungrateful and wicked. (Luke 6:34-35)

What does all this mean when someone comes and asks you for a loan? I think there are the following implications. First, people have an obligation to meet the needs of others within their community. This begs the question, Who is my neighbor? That question has been asked before: Jesus responded with the parable of the Good Samaritan. His answer is still valid today. The New Testament—the New Covenant—has enlarged the boundary of community.

We have responsibility to meet the needs of anyone who comes across our path. If meeting a need means enabling someone to eat or to have warm clothing or heat in the wintertime, then making a loan with interest is wrong. Non-interest-bearing loans are acceptable; an outright gift is better.

BORROWING: THE OTHER SIDE OF CREDIT

To this point, the discussion on credit has really focused on the role of the lender. But perhaps most of us are more concerned with the role of the *borrower*. Again, we need to distinguish between *production* and *consumption* loans.

In the case of a production loan, borrowing is useful because it enables a producer to create even more value. It's perfectly acceptable to borrow the weeding tool to have a more productive garden. It would also be acceptable for the lending neighbor to lend money instead, which could then be used to rent or buy a tool. The use of credit in this situation stands to benefit all parties concerned. The one difference is that the weeding tool can be returned even if the garden fails; but it is not certain that the money could be returned in the event of failure. The lender would be much more interested in the intended use of the loan where money was involved. Because of this, the amount of control exercised by the lender is apt to be greater in cases where preservation of capital is uncertain.

This, then, is one caveat to borrowing money for productive purposes: It represents the binding of economic interests, where the lender exerts influence over the borrower. The borrower would do well to heed the instruction of Scripture about being unequally yoked in these relationships.

> Do not be yoked together with unbelievers. For what do righteousness and wickedness have in common? Or what fellowship can light have with darkness? (2 Corinthians 6:14)

Being unequally yoked could lead a borrower down an undesired path by a more powerful lender.

WANT IT? CHARGE IT!

Borrowing for consumption is more problematic. Under what circumstances is it appropriate to borrow in order to satisfy some present need or want? Proverbs 22:7 gives us a warning:

> The rich rule over the poor, and the borrower is servant to the lender.

When you borrow to satisfy an immediate need or desire, then the loan must be repaid from future wealth that has yet to be created. This will limit your future consumption and could lead to a perpetual state of need. The borrower finds himself in the unpleasant position of always needing to pay now for consumption in the past.

While I have presented a case for not charging interest on need-based consumption loans, the reality of modern life is that interest is exacted in a mighty way. If you were to borrow $500 a year on a credit card for forty years and never pay off the balance, at the end of those forty years you would owe over $2,000,000. You would have had the satisfaction that came with spending $20,000 but have a debt amounting to one hundred times what you spent.[1] The enormity of the resultant debt is the equivalent of a borrower's enslavement to the lender. The lender will take control of your economic choices. Your work in the future goes for the most part to service the debt. Thus, the economic output of the enslaved goes to the master.

Borrowing for consumption is not necessarily wrong. It's just dangerous. People will often borrow to even out their patterns of consumption throughout life, since there are periods in life where ability to generate income is greater or less than the level of consumption. Borrowing in this case may make some sense—but it can still be dangerous.

So What Should I Do?

Let me try to present some general guidelines that I personally use when approaching the issue of credit.

First of all, we have seen that a distinction can be made between *production loans* and *consumption loans.* Credit used to finance business activities, which creates economic value, is entirely appropriate and consistent with biblical values. Credit is to business like a horse is to the cowboy. It's a great help. However, because of its danger, it is not a good idea for the inexperienced rider to get on a horse and run wild. Using credit to finance a business also takes experience. Therefore I encourage people starting out in business to minimize the use of credit. This may limit the ability to grow as fast as you would like, but new businesses will often outgrow their ability to finance that growth.

Think of financing a business like fueling a fire. Fires that burn hot and fast require a great deal more wood to keep the fire going. In fact, a fire that's "too hot" may burn itself out. The same can be true of business growth. Expanding the scope of your new business will require additional capital, and if it happens too fast, the business may just burn itself out.

Consumer credit—borrowing for consumption—is another issue. Like business credit, consumer credit is not, in and of itself, morally wrong. But greed is. And to the extent that consumer credit enables us to fulfill inappropriate materialistic desires, it can take on a dimension that becomes morally wrong.

There is a danger in always being able to have anything

you want. It can foster an unhealthy self-reliance that crowds out the role of God in our lives. Proverbs 30:8-9 says, "Keep falsehood and lies far from me; give me neither poverty nor riches, but give me only my daily bread. *Otherwise, I may have too much and disown you and say, 'Who is the Lord?'* Or I may become poor and steal, and so dishonor the name of my God" (emphasis added).

Here are some guidelines for the use of consumer credit. As a rule of thumb, it is a good idea to avoid using credit to purchase things that depreciate in value. Taking out a loan for a vacation is an example of what I mean. When the vacation is over, the only thing you have on the asset side of the equation is memories. On the liability side, you are stuck with the debt. The net effect is that you have immediately decreased your net worth by the amount of the debt, and will only see further erosion of your financial position as you pay interest to service that debt.

> *Even paying cash carries an "interest charge," in one manner of speaking.*
>
> ★ ★ ★ ★ ★

Using debt to finance the purchase of a home is an entirely different situation. When you buy a home and finance it with a combination of credit and down payment, you have something on the asset side, namely the house itself. True, you have the mortgage as a liability, but the net effect of the transaction has not decreased your financial position at all. It is true that you will have to pay interest to service this debt. But the net interest cost is really only the difference between what the bank charges you and what you could have earned on the cash you may have paid.

This brings up another important point. Even paying cash carries an "interest charge," in one manner of speaking. If you had that money invested, you would be earning interest on it. Whenever you spend money rather than saving it, you are losing the interest you could have earned on it. So whether you pay cash for a home or finance it with a mortgage, there is an interest cost. More often than not, the interest you pay on a mortgage will be higher than what you would get on a low-risk investment that you could have made, so it's safe to say that financing a house with credit is more expensive than using your own cash—but not as much as you may have originally thought.

I should also point out that even when you rent, you are implicitly paying interest because the landlord will take into account his own interest expense on the mortgage of the property when determining what rents to charge.

Borrowing for a vacation and borrowing for a home are two extreme examples. Vacations have no enduring economic value. Homes generally do. (Many homes will even appreciate in value over time, but there is no guarantee on that. There are literally thousands of cases where people have overextended themselves on the purchase of a house only to see a housing boom go bust. In the end, their equity is completely wiped out. Therefore, caution and moderation should be exercised in the use of credit to finance even a item that is not immediately depreciating in value.)

Between these two extreme examples, there are many others that could be considered. I have found that what people often want to know about is automobile loans. Well, an automobile is definitely a depreciating item. Buy a new car, drive it out of the showroom and around the block a few times. Then try to sell it—and you'll see just how fast they depreciate in value. My first reaction, therefore, is that credit should be avoided to finance the purchase of a car.

But when people buy a car, they are really buying transportation for either themselves or their family. Sometimes the transportation itself is needed to enhance the person's ability to produce value—that is, to enable him to get to work. There are other valid reasons for wanting trustworthy transportation, too.

When we were first married, my wife was finishing her last year of nurse's training. She worked in a hospital on the West Side of Chicago, a tough place to live by any standards. It was, in a perverse sort of way, a very convenient place to put a hospital at that. You'd just shoot someone on one side of the street and then carry them right into the hospital on the other. Ruthie would have to drive to and from that hospital at all different times of day and night. She'd pass through some pretty dangerous neighborhoods in the process. Fortunately, a good car was given to us, and we didn't have to use credit to buy one. But I would not have hesitated to do so if that's what it took to secure safe, reliable transportation for my wife. Frankly, I see my wife and kids as "appreciating items," and I want to do whatever I can to ensure their safety and happiness.

Young people starting out will often find themselves settling down in a part of the country that is some distance from their family. I believe that maintaining family relationships also has value that appreciates over time. Having a safe, reliable, and moderately comfortable car to drive the distance back home is another need that might justify using credit to purchase a car.

But credit can also facilitate exercising poor judgment in the purchase of cars. I remember vividly standing in line behind two students at the college union on our campus. They were having a discussion and I, by virtue of my proximity (and admittedly, my natural curiosity), was listening to what they were saying. Their conversation went something like this:

Student #1: "Hey, didn't I see you driving a brand-new red convertible the other day?"

Student #2: "Oh yeah! I love it. It's a graduation gift from my father."

Student #1: "Really? That's awesome. What a great graduation gift!"

Student #2: "Well, it's not really all a gift. Dad made the down payment for me and gave me the coupon book to make the rest of the payments."

That was no inexpensive car. It was sporty. It was *fast*, *fully* equipped, and it was *financed*. And whatever else it was, it was no true gift. I couldn't help but feel sorry for that young student. What kind of lesson was being taught about the use of consumer credit? At that point, the car was getting all the attention. But I knew only too well that it would be the burden of the consumer debt that would distract the student's attention in the days ahead.

When considering the use of credit to finance your next purchase, ask first whether it is a true need or a want. Credit is an expensive way to satisfy wants. It is something that I'd advise people to avoid. Consider also whether or not the item in question has any enduring value or benefit that may justify the use of credit. In short, use credit carefully and wisely, remembering that there are no simple answers to this complex issue.

CHAPTER 3

Mind Your "Mines"

Private property

I LIKE little kids. I especially like them at the crumb-cruncher stage. Crumb-crunchers can be defined by the percentage of food that winds up *on* their person versus *in* their person. Whenever less than 50 percent of food items presented wind up being consumed, a kid is a crumb-cruncher. This is really a precious age, when anything that is wrong in life can be made right by the mere act of having a graham cracker placed in one's hand.

It is sometime during the crumb-cruncher stage of life that people begin expanding their vocabulary. Shortly after developing the capacity to address Mommy, Daddy, and other family members, a child learns to say no. It's as if all humans were programmed with the ability to "just say no" without ever being taught. I find the common advertising theme of "just say no" to drugs, sex, or whatever somewhat amusing—not because there is anything funny at all about abstinence, but because I want to substitute, "Hey, when it comes to drugs, just do like you did when you were a crumb-cruncher!"

In the development of crumb-crunchers, can you guess what is the very next word they learn after *no?* If you haven't already guessed it, just try this little experiment. Go up to a crumb-cruncher and try to take away his graham cracker.

"Mine!"

Mine is another one of those words we don't have to teach kids. They are born with it. They know its meaning and all of its nuances. It's uncanny. It will cause one crumb-cruncher (the hitter) to hit another crumb-cruncher (the hittee) should the hittee violate its meaning and take a toy from the hitter.

A crumb-cruncher can, in fact, get into some serious trouble due to his understanding of "mine." I know this from personal experience in my own crumb-crunching days. My folks were dorm parents, and the first years of my life were spent in a men's dormitory. A dormitory is, in some senses, communal living, where the limits of "mine" are somewhat restricted. My older brother and I were quite used to going from room to room in search of various and sundry "crumbs" to crunch. The college students found this behavior amusing and encouraged it by rewarding us with all sorts of exotic crumbs.

We eventually moved to our own home in a regular neighborhood, where the neighbors had a much more defined sense of the meaning of "mine" than did my brother and I. We didn't know this, however, until we had violated the "mineness" of an elderly neighbor-lady several houses down by entering her house in search of crumbs. She found us in her kitchen, rifling through her cupboards. Unlike the college men in our previous dorm life, she was not at all amused by our behavior and let my mother know this in no uncertain terms.

I was reminded of this incident fairly recently when some crumb-crunchers in our own neighborhood wanted to present me with a bouquet of flowers. That's the good news. The bad news, of course, was that they came from a flower garden I had recently planted and now was virtually no more. But it was OK. I remembered being a crumb-cruncher myself.

While I will admit there is a lot about crumb-crunchers that I find endearing, a crumb-cruncher's attitude and behavior related to the concept of "mine" can often get ugly. One of the worst arguments I ever had with my brother was over a pair of socks. I was sure they were mine; he was absolutely convinced they were not. I lost the argument in arbitration (meaning Mom decided they were my brother's).

But the ugliness of kids arguing about what belongs to whom can look positively pristine when compared to adults arguing about the same issues. It's the stuff that wars are made of. It can make the bitterness of divorce sink to the lowest depths. It can be the seed of feuds between neighbors that endure a lifetime.

It is this ugly side of the issue of "mine" that causes some people to wince when they think about economic systems designed on the principle of private property. Capitalism, as opposed to socialism, is a system where the rights to control both the means of production and economic output belong to private individuals rather than to the state or smaller public units. The right to hold private property—the right of saying, "It's mine"—is at the core of a capitalistic market economy.

Whose Is It, Really?

Property rights have been a source of constant irritation for the human race. God, from the outset, recognized that it would be so and addressed the problem twice in the Ten Commandments.

You shall not steal. (Exodus 20:15)

You shall not covet your neighbor's house. You shall not covet your neighbor's wife, or his manservant or maidservant, his ox or donkey, or anything that belongs to your neighbor. (Exodus 20:17)

The economic significance of these commandments is remarkable. To steal is to take something that does not belong to you. To covet is to want something that does not belong to you. If something does not belong to you, it must logically belong to someone else. If no one else had a right to that property, you couldn't "steal" it. These verses are quite clear about ordaining a system of property rights.

Sometimes we want what other people have and are willing to sin to get it. The apostle James, recognizing our impure motives when it comes to desire for personal gratification, comments on the problems that come from wanting that which belongs to someone else:

What causes fights and quarrels among you? Don't they come from your desires that battle within you? You want something but don't get it. You kill and covet, but you cannot have what you want. You quarrel and fight. You do not have, because you do not ask God. When you ask, you do not receive, because you ask with wrong motives, that you may spend what you get on your pleasures. (James 4:1-3)

One of the main reasons that "owning things" causes such problems for people is that we forget that our claim is really limited to control over *the use of* any property we "own." Everything we have ultimately belongs to God. God is the only one who can legitimately claim, "It's mine."

The earth is the Lord's, and everything in it, the world, and all who live in it. (Psalm 24:1)

While God has the ultimate claim of ownership, he has given to mankind the rights of control over earth's resources (see Genesis 1:27-30, for example). We commonly use the word *stewardship* to describe the relationship of man to the material resources of this world. We appear to have been given a considerable amount of liberty to use the earth's resources as we see fit, with the only proviso being that we use them in a way that would please the owner. Stewards are given the responsibility of acting in the best interest of the principal they represent—a position of great trust.

If every person took seriously the responsibility to exercise property rights from the perspective of pleasing God, the world would look very different than it does today. But people, acting out of either ignorance or disobedience, by and large treat property under their control as if they were the ultimate owner. Seldom does their concern for its use extend beyond mere self-gratification.

WHY DOES IT MATTER?
Deciding what should be done with property is, I believe, at the heart of why God protects property rights in the Ten Commandments. With ownership comes the right to control how property is used and also the opportunity to directly benefit from its use. An owner has an incentive to see to it that the property is put to its best possible use. This is

not the case when no one directly bears the cost of its being used poorly.

The problem of worldwide deforestation is one example. Clear land ownership is the exception rather than the rule throughout much of Africa. In many areas, people do not have permanent possession of land but are granted rights by village leaders to farm particular patches for a limited period. In some countries, such as Burkina Faso, the land is reallocated every few years, effectively destroying any incentive for farmers to invest in the long-term enterprise of tree growing (or in other soil and water conservation efforts).

Tree growing in such societies requires a consensus in the community about the need to grow fuel wood, how to share the work of planting and tending the young trees, and how to divide the wood that is finally produced. Confusion among the people about who would benefit from their efforts makes such programs almost impossible to implement.[1]

The lack of well-defined property rights, while not the only cause, is certainly a contributing factor to the steady and rapid loss of forests throughout the world. But woodlands are not the only natural resource that is harmed by the lack of clearly defined rights.

Some of the worst examples of waste and pollution have come to light with the opening of Eastern Europe, where lack of individual property rights had long been a basic tenet of the political and economic system. Consider the following example documenting the demise of the Aral Sea, an enormous, shallow body of water located in what was once the south-central part of the Soviet Union:

> Shortly after the Communists came to power a decision was made that the Soviet Union should become

self-sufficient in cotton production. This required massive diversions of irrigation water, and most of it has come from the two rivers that feed the Aral, the Amu Darya and the Syr Darya. The inflow to the Aral Sea has been reduced to almost nothing, and as a consequence the Sea has been decreasing rapidly in size. From 1960 to the present [1991], the area of the Sea has diminished 40% and the volume 66%. The exposure of enormous salt bottoms has resulted in devastating salt storms and, accompanied by dramatic climate changes, has significantly changed the ecology of the entire region. Twenty of the 24 fish species native to the Aral have disappeared, and the annual fish catch, which employed 60,000 people in the 1950s, has been reduced to zero.[2]

This is simply one of countless situations where the costs of production clearly surpassed any possible benefits to society. In an atheistic, socialist society, regard for the created order is an unknown or at least an unacknowledged thing. It leads to waste and ruin. To have embarked on the course outlined above would have been disastrous in a market economy, where someone individually recognizes the costs and benefits of resource use. The magnitude of the cost in relation to the potential value of cotton produced would have resulted in enormous losses. With no possibility of profit, resources would simply not have been directed in this way.

> **Property rights and markets make producers accountable for their costs of production.**
> ★ ★ ★ ★ ★

This is not to say that there is never any pollution or waste in a market economy. Indeed there is—and we will touch on some of these problems in later chapters. But the point is well worth making that property rights and markets make producers accountable for their costs of production. The benefit to society from this arrangement is that people become better, albeit not perfect, stewards of the earth's resources.

SO WHAT SHOULD I DO?

When it comes to making economies and markets work, private property is a key ingredient. As important as it is, however, it must be kept in perspective.

Not too long ago, my dad sold the family homestead and moved into an apartment. As a result, Dad had to get rid of a great deal of stuff that our family had accumulated over the years. One of the things he passed on to me was his power lawn mower. I was delighted to have it. Not only was it a power tool, it was a top-of-the-line power tool. It was worth five times what I had spent on my own mower—and better yet, my sons really seemed to enjoy mowing our grass with Grandpa's mower. When your boys like to cut the grass, that means you don't have to, and that I like.

Lawn mowing in our family was working out just splendidly that summer. I beamed with satisfaction as I watched my son mow the lawn. The new mower was gliding along the grass, purring ever so contentedly, when suddenly I heard a *klank-bang,* followed immediately by silence.

This new mower did a great job of cutting grass. It didn't work nearly as well on steel. There is a city water pipe that juts up a few inches from the ground on our parkway. I know where it is, and I'm always careful not to run the mower over that area. My son was not so careful. The result was a bent crankshaft and a three-hundred-dollar repair estimate. That was three times what I had spent for my first lawn mower, which now was my only lawn mower.

I will not claim that I handled this incident perfectly. I *will* claim that I could have done a lot worse. What kept me somewhat in check was the memory of an incident in my own past. It was my sixteenth birthday, and my folks had invited my girlfriend and some family members over for a small celebration on my behalf. The festivities had been delightful, but it was getting to be time to take my girlfriend home. Though she lived only a few blocks away, I wanted to drive her home. I had just that very day received my driver's license, and this was my opportunity to really make an impression. As it turned out, I ended up making two impressions.

The first was on the left front fender of our car. With my girlfriend at my side and my entire family watching me, I carefully backed the car out of the driveway. Fixing all my attention on the rear of the car, I skillfully negotiated our long driveway, reached the end, and began my rear turn out onto the street. I forgot, however, to take any note of what was happening to the front end of the car.

People are always more important than things.

★ ★ ★ ★ ★

There was a telephone pole at the end of our driveway. It had been there for years. It's funny how some things go unnoticed in life until it's too late. I finally noticed this pole when I swung the front end of the car into it.

As you can well imagine, this incident also made an impression on my girlfriend. But it wasn't the kind I had intended.

To say that I was feeling a little bit vulnerable at that moment is to say that Niagara Falls is a little leak on the Canadian-U.S. border. I can't remember what my dad said, but I can remember the way he said it. And the way he said it conveyed to me that the only real issue at that moment was to make sure I understood that I was more important to him than his car.

People are always more important than things. That is what my dad taught me. There was property loss, but the people came out whole. And that's what was really important.

The spirit of the early church in Jerusalem illustrates valuing people over possessions. It shows that the people were more concerned that others' needs were being met than about protecting their property rights.

> All the believers were one in heart and mind. No one claimed that any of his possessions was his own, but they shared everything they had. . . . There were no needy persons among them. For from time to time those who owned lands or houses sold them, brought the money from the sales and put it at the apostles' feet, and it was distributed to anyone as he had need. (Acts 4:32, 34-35)

Incidentally, this example is frequently offered as evidence that property rights did not exist in the early church. That is a mistake. They still existed. Control over the property was merely transferred from individuals within the group to the church as a whole and administered by the apostles.

This matter of transferring control over property was specifically pointed out by Peter as he condemned Ananias for withholding a portion of the proceeds of the sale of his property, pretending that he was turning it all over to the control of the church:

> Peter said, "Ananias, how is it that Satan has so filled your heart that you have lied to the Holy Spirit and have kept for yourself some of the money you received for the land? Didn't it belong to you before it was sold? And after it was sold, wasn't the money at your disposal? What made you think of doing such a thing? You have not lied to men but to God." (Acts 5:3-4)

These early Christians' financial decisions emphasize the true nature of a Christian's relationship to property as one of stewardship. They also show us that, when it comes to deciding what is the best thing to do with money, we would do well to submit ourselves to the counsel of other believers. And finally, they underscore the most important principle of all: People are always more important than things.

CHAPTER 4

Making the Big Buck

The profit motive

DO YOU remember some of your great schemes for making money as a kid? I do. Somewhere along the way, the American rite of passage includes setting up a lemonade stand. We always used Kool-Aid.

Those were the long lazy days of summer. The inspiration would come about 9:00 in the morning. The idea would be followed up by a flurry of activity making plans on how and where to set up our stand. Of course we'd have to have an advertising blitz, which consisted of sending my little brother up and down the neighborhood yelling, *"Kool-Aid . . . Get your ice-cold Kool-Aid . . . Only five cents!"* Then there was product development. We could be quite creative in that arena. We would mix all different kinds of flavors, and when you doubled the amount of sugar called for, it hardly mattered what else you put in. The next thing we did was wait for the business to start pouring in. And we'd wait . . . and wait . . . and wait.

"Look! Here comes someone walking down the street. OK now, everyone start yelling!"

At that point we'd start shouting all of our clever slogans designed to break down the resistance of the toughest consumer. If the unsuspecting soul had pity on us, we would make a sale. Most of the time, however, folks would wind up crossing to the other side of the street just to avoid being accosted by our little Kool-Aid mob. In the end, we'd make very little money and wind up drinking most of the inventory ourselves. (Love that sugar!)

I also tried selling seeds. I remember sending away for my box of inventory. It came in January. January in Chicago can get pretty cold and the snow can be deep. But the weather did little to dampen my enthusiasm, so I donned my winter woolens and, armed with optimism, trudged off to sell my seeds. I went up to the frozen front porch of a house and rang the doorbell. An elderly gentleman came to the door and found me there loaded with my box and my pitch.

"Do you want to buy some seeds, mister?" (What a clever opening!)

"Do I want to buy some *what?*" he responded.

"Seeds, mister. Wouldn't you like to buy some seeds?" I put on my best seed-selling smile and proudly held out my box of seeds.

He first looked down at the box in my hand and then he looked up, somewhat incredulously, at the near-blizzard conditions raging outside. "Son, when am I supposed to plant these seeds?" he asked. I responded that I guessed he ought to wait until spring. At that point he abruptly said, "Come back in five months!" and slammed the door.

No doubt you have your own stories on the trials of making money while growing up that underscore the difficulty of earning a profit. These experiences are fun to look back on and may even have been good for us. But there are also stories from our adult years that aren't so funny.

As a CPA, I have had opportunities to learn the stories of several different businesses. I can think of the story of a drywall contractor. It was very tough to make a living hanging drywall. Not only was the work physically demanding, it also took considerable intelligence and craftsmanship to do it right and do it well. What made it particularly difficult for Tom (not his real name) was that he refused to cover up any shoddy framing with drywall. Tom didn't make money because he insisted that all corners should be square. He wanted all edges on soffits to be level—and if they weren't, he'd stop and fix them before proceeding with his own work. He would pull out defective wall studs and replace them with solid ones. Tom could have simply covered these things up, and no one would ever have known the difference. But Tom could not live with that. I saw it come directly out of his profits. The busier the builders would get, the more shortcuts they would take and the more time and energy Tom would spend fixing their work. Eventually, Tom had to quit his business for lack of profits.

> **How do people react to the notion of profits?**
> **I suspect it depends on who is doing the profiting.**
> ★ ★ ★ ★ ★

In one sense, I really wish Tom's drywall business had been more profitable. He is a fine man, has a fine family, and was good at what he did. He deserved better.

There are other businesses that I wish were not doing so well. One and a half million customers a year in the United States make abortion-on-demand a very busy and all-too-profitable industry. The draw of big and easy profits from lotteries, and gaming fever in general, is luring states and municipalities to "cash in" on the gambling epidemic.

How do people react to the notion of profits? I suspect it depends on who is doing the profiting. When it comes to our own profits, we tend to see it as the blessing of God on our work. If, however, other people are the ones making big profits, it somehow becomes easier to find in their profiting some degree of fault, shortcoming, or misguided values.

Our reaction to profit also depends on how those profits were earned. If the object of the business enterprise is socially or culturally acceptable, then successful people (as measured by profits) are often given great respect. Of course, the converse is true if we don't approve of a particular line of business.

There are certainly enough examples on both sides of the profit issue to lead to a general state of confusion about what our attitude should be.

The Story of Good Profits

In a market economy, the ones who make the most profit are those who produce, in an efficient, low-cost manner, those things that society most needs or wants. There are two sides of the profit picture: the price people are willing to pay, and the cost of production.

High prices are obviously good for the seller. And although it is not as obvious, they can also at times be good for buyers. High prices are a clear signal in a market system that lets everyone know that people place a great deal of value on a particular product or service. High prices have a way of rapidly directing producers to allocate resources to the production of that "hot item." Producing highly desired goods and services leads to the kind of pricing opportunities that contribute to a favorable profit picture.

The other side of the profit picture is the cost of production. A low-cost production system means that fewer of society's limited resources are being used up. Firms that are especially good at conserving society's resources in the production process will, at least in theory, be the most profitable. Firms that are wasteful cannot compete and will have to either become more efficient or leave the market. The need to make a profit, then, forces producers to be good stewards of the resources at their command. Stewardship of resources is certainly a value that is consistent with a Judeo-Christian worldview.

Profit, as a major driving force in any market economy, will have the effect of directing resources to the production of goods and services most valued by society.

★ ★ ★ ★ ★

The market also has a way of throwing cold water on the efforts of well-meaning and perhaps careful, efficient producers who want to make things that society doesn't really need or want. The market simply refuses to buy at a price that makes it worthwhile for the producer. This reality puts a check on the amount of resources that can be wasted in the production of unwanted goods and services—another manifestation of good stewardship. Profit, as a major driving force in any market economy, will have the effect of directing resources to the production of goods and services most valued by society.

Producing what society needs and wants at a reasonable price is an application of Golden-Rule living: looking out for the interests of others. While it is, of course, possible to have a less noble motive and still look out for the interests of others, it's nice to think that there is an entire economic system out there that is constantly assessing my needs and wants and looking for ways to satisfy them.

THE STORY OF BAD PROFITS

It's one thing to know what people need and want in order to do a good job of satisfying those needs and wants. It's another thing entirely to use market power and control over resources and distribution to take advantage of people. When market power is unduly concentrated, it enables firms to set unfair prices and provides little incentive for them to keep production costs as low as possible.

In fact, there might even be incentive to knowingly operate at inefficient levels. This would happen if by restricting output and keeping a highly desired product in short supply the firm could then exact a dear price and raise more revenue than it could by selling more units at a lower price. (Of course, this is one area where government gets involved in setting restrictions on economic activity. We'll examine the role of government in the economy in chapter 6.)

The kind of self-serving economic activity that uses market power to eliminate competition and take advantage of society runs counter to Golden-Rule living. Christians have a responsibility to see that the economic environment permits and even encourages the presence of fair competition. Competition increases output, drives down market prices, and forces firms to operate at more efficient levels of production. (We'll look at economic competition in more detail in the next chapter.)

Another source of "bad profits" comes from the market's ability to reward producers for delivering exactly what people want, which we earlier identified as a strength of the market economy. The problem, of course, is that a market system does not discriminate between people's legitimate needs and their sinful desires. Producers who meet either one will be rewarded with profit.

Illicit drugs, pornography, prostitution, and gambling are all examples of destructive products that people want and for which producers are rewarded with handsome profits.

As it turns out, the profits may even be greater in the case of sinful products because the supply is often restricted by law or moral persuasion. The restricted supply allows producers to earn unusually high profits. Ordinarily, the profits would attract other producers to the market, but it does not necessarily happen in this case. Many potential producers are reluctant to enter this market because they morally object to what is being produced or they are afraid of possible legal sanctions. In the case of organized crime, there may even be life-threatening implications for becoming a producer in a given market.

When a culture becomes increasingly pluralistic to the point where Judeo-Christian values are no longer the norm, there is no reason to expect moral restraint in the marketplace. The market will become adept at meeting the sinful desires of people; the profit motive will ensure that it happens.

Herein lies a dilemma. Profit in the marketplace is fundamentally a good force, helping to direct resources in an efficient way to meet society's needs and wants. But that same force will hasten the moral destruction of society when godly values are no longer widely accepted.

When a culture becomes increasingly pluralistic to the point where Judeo-Christian values are no longer the norm, there is no reason to expect moral restraint in the marketplace. The market will become adept at meeting the sinful desires of people; the profit motive will ensure that it happens.

★ ★ ★ ★ ★

So What Should I Do?

Christians need to accept the challenge of being salt and light, to counter the trend in society away from godly values. Salt is the preservative that keeps the system from decay. As Christians, we "salt" the system whenever we make choices as to what we buy or in what we invest. We should also be light and show others that there is a better way. People are sinners, and sinners love darkness rather than light. But still, people are also made in the image of God and have a God-made conscience that responds to moral truth. It is the business of light to let the moral truth of God shine so that it illuminates the sin in people's lives. To the extent that the church responds to its mission, we can expect the profit motive to accomplish great good in society. If the church fails, the profit motive will hasten society's moral decay.

> **To the extent that the church responds to its mission, we can expect the profit motive to accomplish great good in society.**
>
> ★ ★ ★ ★ ★

For a Christian, the pursuit of profit can be a noble endeavor. To pursue profit is to look for and engage in economic opportunities that offer the greatest potential for the creation of value, in a way that consumes the least amount of economic resources. Are you in business? Setting profit goals in your business is a good idea. The goal will provide the motivation that is needed to continually examine the value-creating efforts of the business. It forces you to ask, Are we doing the right things in the right way?

If you are not making a profit, it's worth asking why. It could be that you are not producing things that society values. This may or may not be a bad thing. As we have seen, society's values often run counter to God's values—and that may be why the world places so little value on what you produce. But it may also be true that you are not producing the "right things" with the economic resources that are under your control. Resources are scarce and should not be wasted on things that do not have an appropriate use in the world.

Another reason for a lack of profits may be inefficient or wasteful operating procedures. Companies can take on the characteristics of people in this regard. People can be wasteful in spending their own resources and can very well bring this propensity with them to the workplace.

If you *are* making a profit, it is important to reflect on how you're doing it. Thoughtful Christians will understand that market power can be abused. Are you engaging in unfair or unethical practices? Is your product or service one that caters only to people's sinful desires, or one that meets a legitimate need? Are you taking advantage of people or businesses that are under your control? If not—if the game was fair and your product or service has true merit—then accept profit as evidence of a job well done.

CHAPTER 5

It's a Jungle Out There

Economic competition

A STUDENT came to my office one day, somewhat distressed by the fact that he was behind in his class work. He had been ill and, as a result, had missed some classes. I tried to accommodate the student as best I could, but I also suggested that he try to borrow another student's class notes to catch up on what he had missed. I was appalled by what I heard next. This student had already approached another in class who did a good job of taking notes. His request was denied on the grounds that it might serve to undermine the note-taker's grade by enabling the student who had been ill to get a higher grade on the upcoming exam.

An article in the *Wall Street Journal* in July 1994 reported on a lawsuit between rival airlines. An airline executive who had been recruited away to join another airline was discovered to have sensitive and valuable data in his possession that was the intellectual property of his former employer. When asked how it came into his possession, he allegedly said he must have inadvertently brought it with him when he left his former job. It was later discovered that the information, which was recorded on a computer diskette, was not copied onto the diskette until two months after the executive had left his former employer. Further investigation revealed that the information was copied and sent to the executive by another employee who was, allegedly, asked to do so shortly before leaving that same former airline for a new job at the airline in question. This employee repeatedly denied that she *"brought"* the information with her to her new job—only to later admit that she had actually *"sent"* it by Express Mail. The airline acting as plaintiff in the suit is seeking $50 million or more in actual damages, an injunction barring its rival from use of the information, and an unspecified amount in exemplary damages.[1]

> **A free-market economy is, by definition, an economy where the forces of unbridled competition are totally unleashed.**
>
> ★ ★ ★ ★ ★

I don't know about you, but stories like these make me angry. Yet competition is a pervasive element of our society. In a democracy, ideas compete against one another. We certainly have our share of common proverbs on the idea of competition:

"It's a jungle out there!"

"We live in a dog-eat-dog kind of a world!"

"In business, it all boils down to survival of the fittest!"

"Winning isn't everything, it's the only thing!"

"Our goal is simply to be the best!"

These phrases all reflect the ever-present reality that we live in a world where competition, of all sorts, is an integral part of the fabric of society.

Economic competition is also a major force in the modern market economy. A free-market economy is, by definition, an economy where the forces of unbridled competition are totally unleashed.

Economists work from a basic proposition that all resources are scarce. The labor pool is only so big. There is
only a fixed amount of land. We have a limited supply of
fossil fuels. We do not have infinite deposits of minerals.
Competition for scarce resources is the heart of the economic problem.

Competition has historically brought out the best and
the worst in human beings. It is the negative aspects, all
too familiar to us, that tend to make many people uncomfortable with, if not outright opposed to, competition. Is
competition compatible with a Christian worldview?

WE CAN DO BETTER

I can remember one summer vacation when our family
had rented a cabin by a lake in northern Wisconsin. I had
been out on a rowboat for some time and hadn't noticed
that the weather had taken a turn for the worse. It was a
fairly dramatic change and brought with it a strong wind
from out of the southwest. By the time I decided to head
back, the wind and waves were pressing hard against me.
Nevertheless, putting my back to the task, I began rowing
into the wind. I went at it for some time, working hard
and concentrating on my rowing. When I looked up and
saw the shoreline, I was shocked and sorely disappointed
by the lack of progress I had made. The distance between
my boat and the shoreline was virtually the same as it had
been when I began my work. I was, in fact, having trouble
simply maintaining my current position and not being
blown further away from my intended destination.

I was in a bit of a quandary. I had, after all, been working
hard and staying very focused on my efforts. But the shoreline, serving as an objective point of reference, didn't lie. I was

going nowhere. It became painfully clear to me that if I was ever to get back home, I needed to do more than I was doing.

It is human nature to perceive that our accomplishments are more substantial than they really are. We are well served when we have an objective measure for judging where we stand that lets us know that we need to do better. This is one useful outcome of competition. We need only look to our competition to see if we can do better.

Let me ask the following questions in support of my argument:

- Is the quality of American cars better or worse as a result of Japanese competition?
- Are personal computers cheaper or more expensive because of the variety of clones?
- Has the Apple computer's popularity made your non-Apple PC easier or more difficult to work with?
- Would you enjoy the variety of services that you get from your local bank or credit union if it were the only financial institution in town?
- Would you have the same selection of goods and choice of hours to shop if there were only one food store in town?
- How many Bibles do you have? How many different versions do you consult when you're into some serious Bible study? Do you think you'd have the same breadth of supplements, such as notes, maps, concordances and the like, if there were just one Bible publishing house?

The benefit of competition is that it stimulates us to set our sights higher. It provides us with a challenge to do better than we are doing. It ultimately serves to provide society with higher-quality goods that serve us better. It adds diversity and makes life more interesting. It often forces us to learn how to do more with less cost and less harm to the environment. It promotes, in general, a higher level of economic welfare. These things, I believe, are pleasing to God.

WHY THE TOWER OF BABEL WAS A GOOD IDEA

I must admit I've thought a lot about the Tower of Babel and the difficulties that it has brought upon the human race as people of different language groups throughout the world interact with each other in a variety of contexts. It would certainly be much easier if we all spoke the same language. Was there any good that came from confusing peoples' language? Genesis 11:6 reads,

> The Lord said, "If as one people speaking the same language they have begun to do this, then nothing they plan to do will be impossible for them."

What God did in this case was step in and break up the concentrated power of a cohesive, well-organized group of people. If mankind's purposes were always noble, then I don't believe God would mind such social organizations. But the truth is that the desires of our heart often run counter to God's. When God stepped in and divided mankind into distinct language groups, he provided a natural division of power. Throughout the ages, differing people groups have acted as checks and balances on each other. One group has acted as a restraint on the evil of another.

Competition in the economic sphere serves this same purpose. If you think about it, most of the economic injustice we see in the world is caused not by competition, but rather by the lack of it. Extreme concentration of economic power is used more often to exploit than to help people. This is the reason we have an extensively developed public policy of antitrust. Insider trading, price fixing, predatory pricing, dumping, collusion, and cartel formation are all activities that reduce economic competition.

> **Competition serves as a measure of restraint on the exploitation and oppression that comes from concentrated economic power.**
>
> ★ ★ ★ ★ ★

Competition serves as a measure of restraint on the exploitation and oppression that come from concentrated economic power. This benefit is not trivial and is certainly in keeping with the spirit of God's response to the Tower of Babel.

COMPETITIVE MARKETS AND A BIGGER PIE

Societies must decide what kind of system will be used to allocate their resources. The world is moving increasingly and in dramatic fashion to a system of competitive markets to organize its economic production and distribution. The reason for this is the overwhelming evidence that markets have done a better job of producing goods and services for society than have systems designed around centralized planning.

People tend to misconstrue what it means to be competitive in an economic setting. In competitive athletic events, there are winners and losers, champions and everybody else. In politics, competitive democratic elections also result in winners and losers.

But the same reasoning cannot be applied to competitive markets. Competitive markets are characterized by *many* "winners," each participating in a dynamic process that leads to an expanding economic pie. Competition in markets is *inclusive*, not exclusive. Equal opportunity to participate in economic activity is at the very essence of what it means for a market to be competitive.

It is an incorrect stereotype that portrays competitive economic activity as a zero-sum endeavor, where a gain for one side always entails a corresponding loss for the other side. If management wins, then labor must lose. If the owners of a company get rich, then the company's employees or customers must be worse off.

In a system that is governed by voluntary exchange, economic activity will only occur when *each party* perceives itself as benefitting by the exchange. This voluntary exchange will lead to higher levels of economic welfare for all parties choosing to enter into the exchange.

What happens when you buy a car? You walk into the dealership committed to not paying one dime more than the car is worth. The dealer, on the other hand, is equally committed to selling that car for its full market value. When negotiations are completed, you trade money for the car. You're happy and consider yourself "better off" than when you had the money but no car. The dealer is happy and considers himself better off with the money than when he had the car. Both parties agreed to the price of the item being exchanged, and yet both walk away better off than they were prior to the exchange.

The same thing happens when employers exchange money for an employee's time and effort. Each agrees to the price (wage) associated with the effort exchanged, and each party considers itself better off than if the exchange did not occur.

Economic activity, characterized by voluntary exchange, is a value-creating process. It is not a zero-sum activity where, in order for someone to win, someone must lose. While we recognized earlier that competition has its roots in the limited nature of valuable resources, that still doesn't mean that there must be winners and losers in the game. The exchange process is a way of combining scarce resources to create things of value greater than the sum of their parts, resulting in a net benefit to everyone involved in the exchange.

COMPETITION AND INDIVIDUALISM

Individualized responsibility, accountability, and rewards are integral parts of a market-oriented economy. Centralized, cooperative, or government-controlled economies, by contrast, are built around group responsibility, group accountability, and shared rewards.

Competition naturally grows out of a strong emphasis on the role of the individual in society. In considering the merits of economic competition, it would be prudent to consider individualism from a Christian perspective.

The Bible teaches that each of us is responsible and ultimately accountable for our own actions. Salvation is a particularly individualized matter. I am saved by no one's faith but my own. As we will see in a moment, individualism is by no means the *only* Christian value or norm to be followed in every social structure. But individual responsibility and reward are modeled in Scripture in some circumstances.

In a market economy, economic competition will direct the most rewards to those participants that do the best job of meeting the needs and wants of the society. Differentiation in rewards based on performance is consistent with biblical teaching that each man will be judged according to his works. Differentiating rewards does not necessarily lead to an unjust outcome. Consider school, for instance. In the catalog for the college where I teach, we say:

> Grades are given for passing work, with significance as follows: A, distinctive; A-, B+, B, superior; B-, C+, C, acceptable; C-, D, inadequate.

To ignore individual performance and evaluation would force us into giving one grade to an entire class or even to the entire school. Ignoring differences in accomplishment between members in the group is generally accepted as unjust. We all have our own stories of how our accomplishments in the workplace have sometimes gone unnoticed and unrewarded. The wrong that comes from failure to adequately distinguish between accomplishment and contribution is indeed real.

INDIVIDUALISM AND COMMUNITY—
A TOUGH ACT TO BALANCE
The greatest problem with individualism as manifested through economic competition is that too often we lose sight of our responsibilities as individuals to the community at large. Consider Ecclesiastes 4:4:

> All labor and all achievement spring from man's envy of his neighbor. This too is meaningless, a chasing after the wind.

This text, though written many centuries ago, is relevant today. It points to one of the main reasons people are concerned about the principle of competition: We have all observed at some time that a person's demonstration of skill or effort is motivated by jealous rivalry. The intent is to outdo another for the sake of lifting oneself up or putting the other person down. This is vanity. Competition can be carried out in a way that is destructive to others, and this is displeasing to Christ. Christians need to recognize this potential pitfall in competition.

One way to salt competitive economic life is to appreciate the spirit of cooperation that is central to the concept of community. While Scripture clearly exhibits patterns of individual responsibility, accountability, and rewards, the Bible also frequently depicts patterns of group responsibility, group accountability, and shared rewards. Reflect for a moment if you will on God's many promises to the nation of Israel in the Old Testament. His judgment and blessing was meted out on the nation as a collective unit. Consider also God's words to the seven churches in the book of Revelation. Each church was addressed as a body of believers. Clearly, God is concerned about believers not only in an individual sense, but also as a community of faith.

> Two are better than one, because they have a good return for their work: If one falls down, his friend can help him up. But pity the man who falls and has no one to help him up! (Ecclesiastes 4:9-10)

There is often real merit in organizing economic enterprise on the basis of partnership. The imagery is one of people working together for a common goal that in turn leads to the betterment of all.

So What Should I Do?

The department manager called his staff into the conference room. On the wall, there was a wide sheet of paper stretching from floor to ceiling. The manager gave each staff member a marker and asked them each to make a mark on the paper as high as they possibly could.

When they had all finished, the manager stared at the paper silently for a moment. Then, with a knowing smile, he turned to his staff members and asked them to do it again. This time, they were to make their mark higher. Without exception, they were able to surpass their original marks—which had supposedly been as high as they could reach.

What enabled them to do better the second time? It was the first mark.

The first mark gave each employee a reference point and a goal. In order to do better, you need to first know how well you are doing.

One of the most significant benefits of competition is that it offers us an unbiased reference point on how we are doing in life. One key element of the "quality movement" in U.S. industry today is the idea of setting a benchmark. The idea is that you look at the high-quality firms in your industry to set the standard, or benchmark if you will, by which to evaluate your own performance. In order for this to have any positive effect, you need to look for competitors that are doing better than you are. Comparisons with low-quality producers will do nothing to improve your own position.

Looking to your high-quality competitors is one way to establish a reference point on how well you are doing. The other place to go is to your customers. Ask them how you are doing. Ask them how you can improve. Quality improvement necessitates caring about your customers. If you don't, they will eventually go to someone who does.

I have found the principle of setting a benchmark to be very useful in a personal way. I am a teacher and I try to look at the best teachers I can find and then use them as a reference point to improve my own work. It can also be useful as a tool to stimulate personal spiritual growth. Much of the personal motivation for developing disciplines in prayer, Bible study, evangelism, service, and stewardship has come from watching and relating to Christians who are farther along than I am in spiritual disciplines of life.

> **Look for people who can make you better, not complacent. And remember, the ultimate benchmark is Jesus.**
>
> ★ ★ ★ ★ ★

Do you ever wish you had a better prayer life? Spend some time with someone who regularly prays, and you will learn from that person. The most excited I have ever been about evangelism was when I met regularly for lunch with an attorney who made witnessing a high priority in his life. In the New Testament, discipling is a near equivalent to the principle of setting a benchmark.

I must emphasize that this is a conscious choice, and one that runs counter to my sinful nature. My natural tendency in this regard is to look around, in judgmental fashion, for those who are "worse" than I am. I am prone to act like that Pharisee who prayed in the temple, "God, I thank you that I am not like other men—robbers, evildoers, adulterers—or even like this tax collector" (Luke 18:11).

Look for people who can make you better, not complacent. And remember, the ultimate benchmark is Jesus.

CHAPTER 6

Should the Word *Government* Be Capitalized?

Government and the economy

T HE BASEBALL game had ended. The home team had come from behind to win in the bottom of the ninth inning. Forty thousand satisfied fans were rejoicing their way through the stadium exits and heading for home. The city public-transit officials had encouraged the fans to use remote parking and take advantage of public mass-transit trains to shuttle to and from the ballpark. It was a good idea and, under normal circumstances, would have worked very well. But this was not a normal day.

There were two sets of turnstiles that permitted passengers to enter the train platforms. One set was for those who had previously purchased passes to use the system. The other was for those who needed to purchase tickets on the spot.

On that fateful afternoon, the turnstiles designed to accommodate customers with passes were out of service. As a result, the transit authority officials (a quasi-government service) decided that everyone would have to use the line for buying tickets, even if they already had a ticket or a pass. Now I am not exactly sure what percentage of the forty thousand fans had decided to use this train, but it felt like all of them did. Whatever jubilation those fans with passes might have been feeling as a result of the victory was soon burned up in frustration and anger at the obstinacy of the transit officials. The officials were in no hurry. They couldn't have cared less that there was a line blocks long waiting to get through. Only when it looked like the scene would turn ugly and they feared an outbreak of riot did one of them come out of the ticket booth and begin to swiftly admit people with a legitimate ticket or pass onto the train platform. I couldn't help but wonder if the experience would have been the same had the transit company been a private instead of a public venture.

* * *

An accountant working for a company of moderate size noticed that the state had made a mistake in assigning a tax rate for the firm's unemployment tax. The firm corrected the mistake, paid the correct amount of tax on a timely basis, and notified the state. The state failed, however, to take proper action to correct its error and, as a result, determined that the firm had underpaid its tax by around $1,500. The firm again notified the state of its error. The state overlooked the notification and accessed a larger penalty and started the interest clock running on the unpaid balance. This sequence of events repeated itself many times over with the state failing to take corrective action until eventually the interest and proposed penalties grew to well in excess of $100,000. At that point, the state got interested and used its power to take the money directly from the firm's bank account. The state did this even though its agents had repeatedly acknowledged that it was all just the result of a clerical mistake on the part of the state. Even the well-respected, longtime senior U.S. senator found himself powerless to redress the situation of his constituent firm. The only recourse left to the firm was to sue the state, which it did. The firm's position was upheld in district court, and the state was ordered to refund the money. It did nothing. The suit was brought to the appellate court, and again the state was found to be in the wrong—and again it did nothing. Only when the state supreme court ordered the state treasury to refund the money did the state do so. The court failed, however, to award the firm interest on the money that had been wrongfully held by the state for a prolonged period of time. Also, attorney fees to recover the money had to be absorbed by the firm.

* * *

I once had a client with a tricky tax question that dealt with social security benefits. It related to a technical definition of a benefit that required some explanation by the Social Security Administration. I tried for three days to get through by telephone to the SSA. I began calling ten minutes before they opened and used an automatic redial feature in my attempt to connect. When I finally did, the agent heard the word *tax*, immediately disengaged mentally, and told me I would have to deal with the IRS. The problem was that I had already dealt extensively with the IRS, and we had concluded that clarification was needed from the SSA. No matter how hard I tried to communicate this point, the SSA agent refused to give the matter even a token amount of consideration. After I had spent literally hours trying to get through to a real person, this agent of government dismissed my plea for clarification in a matter of moments.

*   *   *

Try this little experiment sometime with your friends. Ask them to write down the first thing that comes into their mind when you say "government." I do this regularly with my economic principles classes. They respond with things like, "too big, deficits, debts, taxes, bureaucracy, inefficiency, regulation." Based on some of my own personal experiences with government, I can see why. No doubt you have your own stories which reenforce these rather negative responses.

What you won't frequently see as a response are things like, "ordained by God, peaceful living, rewarders of good, deserving of honor, respectable, in need of prayer." And yet based upon what Scripture says about government, these are legitimate responses. I have found that I am often lacking a proper balance in my own attitude toward government. I believe that there is a legitimate role for government, but there are some very good reasons for making it a limited role. This means I would not spell *government* with a capital *G*. It does not mean, however, that the word should be eliminated entirely from our vocabulary.

> **Try this little experiment sometime with your friends. Ask them to write down the first thing that comes into their mind when you say "government."**
>
> ★ ★ ★ ★ ★

The fact is that no economy operates in a vacuum with respect to government. Economics and government stand side by side and interact with each other in important ways.

It seems that the feelings of the church toward government have always been mixed. There has often been confusion as to what our attitude and interaction with governing institutions should be. Scripture addresses the matter on several occasions with direct teaching about the role of government and how people should respond to it. Consider the following passages:

> Everyone must submit himself to the governing authorities, for there is no authority except that which God has established. The authorities that exist have been established by God. Consequently, he who rebels against the authority is rebelling against what God has instituted, and those who do so will bring judgment on themselves. For rulers hold no terror for those who do right, but for those who do wrong. Do you want to be free from fear of the one in authority? Then do what is right and he will commend you. For he is God's servant to do you good. But if you do wrong, be afraid, for he does not bear the sword for nothing. He is God's servant, an agent of wrath to bring punishment on the wrongdoer. Therefore, it is necessary to submit to the authorities, not only because of possible punishment but also because of conscience. This is also why you pay taxes, for the authorities are God's servants, who give their full time to governing. Give everyone what you owe him: If you owe taxes, pay taxes; if revenue, then revenue; if respect, then respect; if honor, then honor. (Romans 13:1-7)

> Remind the people to be subject to rulers and authorities, to be obedient, to be ready to do whatever is good. (Titus 3:1)

> Submit yourselves for the Lord's sake to every authority instituted among men: whether to the king, as the supreme authority, or to governors, who are sent by

him to punish those who do wrong and to commend those who do right. (1 Peter 2:13-14)

These passages all recognize that government has a legitimate role in the affairs of society. That role includes general enforcement of law, which leads to ordered, peaceful, dignified existence. Government, in this sense, is an honorable institution worthy of our support—financial support in the form of paying taxes, as well as prayer support.

While it seems clear that Scripture recognizes a legitimate role for government and that the church should generally be supportive of it, many of today's pressing questions about the complex, massive government sectors of modern nation-states are not specifically addressed. We must use the principles presented in the totality of Scripture to guide our understanding in these matters.

What are these pressing questions about the role of government? Since this book is about economics, the questions addressed here will be economic ones. What are the various roles of government in the context of a market system? What part do taxes play? Is debt a good thing or a bad thing for government?

Scripture teaches that governments have the authority to correct wrongdoing, keep the peace, and promote order in society. To the extent that the economic system permits or engages in evil practices or outcomes, I believe it is the role of government to intervene and see that justice is served. What kinds of things can go wrong in a market economy?

PLEASE LAND ON BOARDWALK
One thing that can go wrong is for market power to become too concentrated. This concentration of power can

be used to take advantage of society. We even have a word for it and a game modeled after its principles. It's called Monopoly. Let's face it: If you own Boardwalk with a hotel, you can't wait for another player to land on it. At least when I'm in that situation, I desperately hope that the other players will fall into my hands by landing on my monopoly!

While it's just a game, unfortunately the real thing has played the same way often enough that we understand the potential abuse of concentrated market power. One legitimate role of government, then, is to ensure that the economic game is fair by dealing with concentrated market power. In the United States, this role falls to the Justice Department and its Antitrust division.

The best way to prevent concentrated economic power is to find ways of allowing everyone to enter the game. To the extent that people and firms are allowed to become full participants in the economic arena, market forces will tend to lead to outcomes where goods and services are produced at low costs, are in ample supply, and are sold for relatively low prices. Employment levels and total earnings of all workers will also be higher when concentrated economic power does not exist in the labor markets.

We should note that in some cases, it does seem best to allow monopolies to exist because it is more cost-efficient to do so. For example, how many electric utilities does one community need? Do we really want more than one company stringing electric power lines down our streets? No; it would be a waste of resources. In situations like this, market power is concentrated into the hands of one firm, and society then relies on state regulatory commissions to oversee the rates being charged by that utility. These are also joined by citizens' "watchdog" groups that keep an attentive eye on the entire process.

Governments have in the past chosen two ways of dealing with the issue of inappropriate monopolies. One way is *reactive*, and the other is *proactive*. The breaking up of AT&T into smaller companies is an example of a government *reaction* to perceived concentrated economic power. On the *proactive* side, public education is an example of a government institution being used to try to encourage full participation in the economic sector. The Small Business Association is another example of a proactive government institution: It is designed to supply financing to small businesses and give them a chance to participate in the economic arena.

> **Government does have an interventionary role in a market economy to deal with abuses that result from concentrated market power. Obviously, governments have not always been successful in this regard.**
>
> ★ ★ ★ ★ ★

In theory, then, government does have an interventionary role in a market economy to deal with abuses that result from concentrated market power. Obviously, governments have not always been successful in this regard, nor have they always gone about it in the right way. But it is a legitimate role for government to fill.

COUNTING ALL THE COSTS

Concentrated market power is one thing that can go wrong in a market economy. Another thing that can go wrong is that producers don't always take responsibility for all of the production costs they incur. In a normal situation, the marketplace will hold producers accountable for costs of production. If producers don't control their uses of resources and consequently operate at cost levels that are too high, then competition will drive them out of business. There are production costs, though, that are harder to track.

The best example is pollution. If a producer emits pollutants into the air or discharges untreated waste directly into a lake or river, it is the public that suffers from these actions. In the case of acid rain, the ones who bear the cost are often located as far as a thousand miles away from the source.

The case of pollution represents a classic example of market failure. The market fails in the sense that it doesn't fully take into account all production costs. Products that appear profitable—and thus seem to represent a net benefit to society—may in fact be unprofitable, representing a net loss when the costs of pollution are included.

Two questions arise at this point. Is pollution a moral wrong that needs correction? If so, does government have a role in correcting this wrong? The answer to both questions, I believe, is yes. Is it wrong to take something from somebody without their permission? Of course. When a producer pollutes the air or a body of water, something is being given up. A cost is being incurred. It may be that people are giving up the possibility of breathing clean, nontoxic air. It may be that recreational opportunities are being lost to fouled water. This is all being done without the permission of the ones suffering the loss. The cost of pollution is generally something that is absorbed by the public. It is natural, then, to look to government to address this issue because of its position in representing the interests of the public.

Doing the Right Thing

Concentrated market power and not taking responsibility for all production costs are two wrongs that occur in market economies. These present opportunities for governments to take corrective action on behalf of society. These might be considered wrongs of *commission* on the part of a market system. But there are also possibilities for wrongs of *omission*. Failure to do the right thing can be regarded as a wrong.

> Anyone, then, who knows the good he ought to do and doesn't do it, sins. (James 4:17)

This, of course, refers to an individual and not to a government. But it does clearly teach a principle of doing good when one is knowingly given the opportunity to do so. It is considered wrong not to do so. This does seem to at least raise the possibility of government's taking a *proactive* approach in its involvement in the economic affairs of society. But the "good" choice, when it comes to economics, is not always obvious. Frequently it becomes a hotly contested political issue.

Is it good to raise taxes—or to lower them? Is guaranteeing a steady income good, and, if so, what should that guaranteed amount be? Is it good to have a minimum wage? Are rent controls good? Is protecting domestic jobs—through the use of protective tariffs and import quotas—good? Is subsidizing the production of tobacco good? These all tend to be examples of government actions that are intended, at least in someone's mind, to do good. Yet there is little agreement as to the rightness of these actions. Government involvement in these matters is at best problematic.

Government is in one respect no different from any other

institution in society: Government is a group of people. It is true that these people are empowered with authority and bear responsibility to govern the affairs of other people. But like any group, it will make decisions based upon a system of values. Representative government will, overall, reflect the values of those it represents. Authoritarian governments will reflect the values of individuals in authority, values that may or may not be widely held by society. What is deemed "good" will depend on the value system being reflected in the government.

To the extent that society or those in government embrace Judeo-Christian values, governments will be able to discern the "right" thing to do. These actions can be supported in good conscience. But the converse is also true. This is not a very satisfying answer to the question of the role of government. It is not clean, clearcut, or definitive. It seems to leave the matter of the role of government suspect.

It does, however, leave us with one useful result. To take an extremist position with respect to the role of government is unwise. It is clear that governments cannot always be trusted to discern the right thing to do. But it is equally clear that there is no reason to conclude that government *cannot* discern the morally correct thing to do. Sometimes it will, and sometimes it won't. To categorically write off any government action as incapable of accomplishing good is unwise. To embrace government as the means for solving all problems is equally unwise.

Sometimes we can support the actions of government

> *To categorically write off any government action as incapable of accomplishing good is unwise. To embrace government as the means for solving all problems is equally unwise.*
>
> ★ ★ ★ ★ ★

with the full moral authority that comes with knowing and doing what is right. Other times, the actions of government cannot be supported because the choices of people in government to do what is good in their eyes will in reality have morally wrong results.

COUNTING ALL THE BENEFITS

Where does this leave us with respect to the James 4:17 principle of doing good? May I suggest that there are some things that most people will agree make society better off when we have them than when we don't. Furthermore, the benefit to society from having these things exceeds their cost. But if left to market forces alone, these types of things would generally get underproduced.

Consider, for example, the extensive system of highways and bridges throughout the United States. Can you conceive of the same system being developed by a private producer? It is doubtful that it would happen. Collecting user fees from everyone would present an exceedingly difficult task. You would have to have all accesses to the system controlled with toll-collecting mechanisms. The cost to a private firm for producing and selling a road or bridge would be overwhelming, leaving insufficient profit potential to attract investors. Markets would not supply enough highways.

Public education is another example. Unlike a highway system, education can easily be provided for some and not for others. Systems of private education for a privileged few have existed for thousands of years. It has been obvious to many that they will profit from their own education. But what is less obvious is that an individual can be better off when others around him are also educated. There is a synergistic gain from educating a society as a whole that becomes greater than the sum of the personal gains to each educated individual.

Markets in and of themselves will tend to underproduce products like education because would-be buyers only take into account the direct benefit to themselves. People don't calculate and include the benefit to society when they assign a value to whatever it is that they are buying. In short, they are generally willing to pay only for the benefit they receive directly—not for any additional benefit that might flow to society as a whole. This is why markets underproduce goods like education.

In the case of the highway system and public education, society is better off with them than without. Government is in a good position to provide them.

How Big Should Government Be?

I have tried to make a case for the legitimate role of government. Yet given a choice between having goods and services produced either by markets or by government institutions, we must recognize that markets have a structural advantage for doing things better than government. (I emphasize the words *structural advantage*. It has nothing inherently to do with the motivations, abilities, or efforts of people in government as compared to the private sector.) Let me illustrate.

If a business decides to produce something that society does not need or want, it will do so only for a limited period of time. People will not buy things that they do not value. If a firm persists in producing unwanted things, it will waste its capital and find itself in the unhappy position of being unable to attract additional sources of funds. The marketplace will not continually fund losing propositions.

Governments, on the other hand, can produce things on which society, as a whole, places very little value. The costs for these things may far exceed any societal value produced. They become, in fact, losing propositions from society's point of view. But because governments have the power to tax, there is not the same constraint to the further funding of "loser" projects. The losses can continue indefinitely.

A second factor in favor of market production is that, when markets are competitive, there are forces that tend to drive production to its lowest cost. Firms with the greatest success in the market do the best job of efficiently creating value. The firms that cannot compete efficiently will not survive.

Markets have a nasty way of disciplining firms that make poor choices. Businesses cannot ignore the corrective signals in the marketplace and hope to remain in existence. Make something that society doesn't want, and the market lets you know. Produce things of low quality, using inefficient means of production, and the work goes to your competitors.

Monopoly, whether state or private, is a bad idea because the lack of competition breeds complacency and inefficiency.

★ ★ ★ ★ ★

Government production of goods and services, however, generally results in state-run monopolies. Monopoly, whether state or private, is a bad idea because the lack of competition breeds complacency and inefficiency. There is no benchmark to let society know if the monopoly is doing things in the most efficient manner. How are we to know if decisions are good or bad when there is no point of reference in an industry with several other producers?

Markets have one more advantage over government, and that is timely and accurate feedback. Prices—what consumers are willing to pay—are terrific signals to let producers know what should or should not be produced. High prices let the business community know that people place a high value on the output. Low prices encourage producers to shift resources to the production of other goods and services that command higher prices and thus create more value.

What is the price of a road, a space station, a man on the moon, a battleship, or a high-energy physics research project? We can estimate their cost—but that's not the same thing as saying we can estimate their price. Price has to do with the *value created*. Cost is simply the *value of the resources used up* in producing the good or service. Sadly, the two are often confused to the point where government can perversely believe it is actually creating more value by using more resources and incurring more cost.

That is, in fact, how government's contribution to gross national product is measured. In contrast to the private sector, where output is measured in terms of the value of goods and services produced, government's contribution to GNP is measured in terms of how much it spends. The issue of value creation is ignored. This is not the result of some conspiracy on the part of government officials. It is the natural consequence of not having prices, i.e., consumer feedback, available for so many of the kinds of goods and services that governments produce.

Unfortunately this does not leave us with any definitive answer for the question on the size and scope of government. It does, however, provide us with principles to help with the formation of policy. If given the choice between producing goods and services using government monopolies or using market systems of production, *markets have definite advantages.* They provide society with built-in checks and balances to help direct resources to the efficient production of goods and services that society values most. Mistakes in the marketplace will not systematically go unnoticed or undisciplined. When given a choice, choose markets.

GOVERNMENTS AND TAXATION

Scripture does give us some limited but direct teaching on the payment of taxes to a government. When the scribes and chief priests queried Jesus on this matter they asked, "Is it right for us to pay taxes to Caesar or not?" (Luke 20:22). Jesus answered them by asking to see a Roman coin, which had Caesar's inscription and likeness on it. He then said, "Give to Caesar what is Caesar's, and to God what is God's" (Luke 20:25).

On this and several other occasions, Scripture legitimizes the payment of taxes. If the issue is so easily settled, why do people often become so emotionally embroiled in the mundane matters of taxation? The answer is that taxes in the United States have served as a powerful tool that government has used to direct social policy. Our government has used the tax laws to subsidize home ownership, to subsidize investment in historical structures, to subsidize pollution control, to subsidize agriculture, to subsidize parenthood, to subsidize hiring special classes of people, and the list goes on and on. These are not direct subsidies, where payments come straight from the Treasury Department. But they have exactly the same effect of putting money into the pocket of a taxpayer by giving deductions or credits that ultimately reduce the tax bill.

It is the power of taxes to influence outcomes in society

that gives taxation its moral overtones. This aspect of taxation should be regarded just as any other government program with respect to its moral correctness: Sometimes government will do the right thing, sometimes it won't. Taxes have also been used to deal with matters of distributive justice, primarily income redistribution. Many people see a progressive income-tax system, where people pay progressively larger proportions of tax on increasing levels of their income, as a tool to redistribute income. Consider the following example.

A billionaire was out on his yacht when a gust of wind came along and blew a $100 bill from his pocket, carrying it along to where it landed at the feet of a young, poor, unemployed, widowed mother with three sick children. To her it seemed as if a gift had descended from heaven. Would the world be better off, worse off, or unchanged as a result? Many would say that the welfare of the world has somehow increased, arguing that what was gained by the poor mother in need was greater than what was lost by the billionaire in his plenty. As such, they believe that this type of income redistribution is one of those good things that governments ought to be doing.

Scripture's teaching on taxation is not nearly this specific. Scripture does teach that those with means have a responsibility to help the poor. One way of meeting that responsibility, in part, is to use the income-tax system to redistribute income. This does not mean that this is necessarily the role of government, or if it were, that the tax system is the only or best way of accomplishing this goal.

A few bits of actual data from U.S. experience might give some insight as to the current position of the country with respect to who pays taxes. If you split all taxpayers into five groups according to levels of income, for 1992 you would

**PERCENTAGE OF TOTAL TAXES PAID BY
VARIOUS INCOME GROUPS**

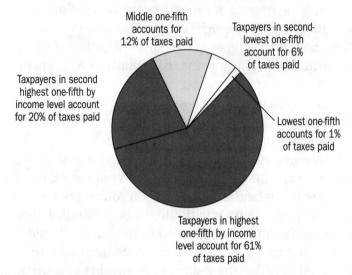

Middle one-fifth accounts for 12% of taxes paid

Taxpayers in second-lowest one-fifth account for 6% of taxes paid

Taxpayers in second highest one-fifth by income level account for 20% of taxes paid

Lowest one-fifth accounts for 1% of taxes paid

Taxpayers in highest one-fifth by income level account for 61% of taxes paid

find that the highest income group paid about 61 percent of all federal taxes collected. The second highest group paid 20 percent of all federal taxes collected. The highest 40 percent income group, then, paid 81 percent of federal taxes. The lowest 40 percent income group paid 7 percent.[1]

I should say parenthetically that one can reject outright the authority of government to redistribute income and still argue for a progressive tax system based upon equity and benefits received. It can be argued that those with wealth or the means to earn large incomes stand to gain more from a stable system of law and order because they have more to protect. Their relatively higher levels of wealth enable them to enjoy more of the goods and services from private and government sectors alike. Because they receive greater benefits, they should pay a higher portion of the cost.

The whole notion of paying for benefits received makes

the matter of paying taxes much more palatable. It seems that in the everyday experience of life, people perceive that public services have little or no cost. We drive on streets, send our children to public schools, drink clean water from a faucet in our home, flush waste away to who-knows-where, fly in airplanes that don't run into each other, buy and sell securities in markets that are remarkably efficient, play in public parks, read books from an abundant selection in a public library, and seldom do we pay, directly, anywhere near the actual cost of what it takes to provide these services.

> **As with individuals, debt for governments is neither inherently bad nor good.**
>
> ★ ★ ★ ★ ★

We pay for these things indirectly through various taxes. Because we don't associate payment of taxes with consuming government services, we don't often absorb the impact of the total value of what government provides to society.

SHOULD GOVERNMENTS GO INTO DEBT?

As with individuals, debt for governments is neither inherently bad nor good. There are good reasons and bad reasons for debt. For individuals, debt that is used to fuel current spending on things that provide only temporary benefits is a dangerous thing. It increases the current standard of living but does so at the expense of a lower future standard of living. People will often do this because they anticipate that their earning power in the future will increase; what they are really trying to do is even out their standard of living over a lifetime. There is, however, no guarantee that future income will indeed be greater, and it is somewhat risky to depend on it.

While it may be imprudent, no one considers it *immoral*

when an individual voluntarily chooses to trade future consumption for present consumption. However, when governments go into debt to raise the current standard of living of society at the expense of future generations, questions of equity, justice, and morality come into play. The current generation is, in fact, taking something from future generations without their consent. The difference is that in the case of the individual, that same individual will personally bear the consequences of faulty judgments or reckless actions. The same cannot be said for intergenerational transfers. It is wrong to take anything from somebody without their consent. It is tantamount to stealing.

> **It is unfair for future generations to expect the current generation to bear all of the cost of something that will provide benefits well into the future.**
>
> ★ ★ ★ ★ ★

But also note this: The same argument can be used in reverse to *justify* government debt. It is unfair for future generations to expect the current generation to bear all of the cost of something that will provide benefits well into the future. Roads, bridges, medical research, systems of defense, education, environmental protection, museums, and libraries are all examples of things that will provide benefits to both current and future generations. Using debt is one way to ensure that all citizens—present and future—share in paying for the benefits they receive. Governments borrow funds on a long-term basis and then use tax revenues from the citizens of the future to retire this debt over the life of the project that it funded.

To summarize, government debt is justified when the proceeds of the debt are used to finance something that provides both current and future benefits to taxpayers. People should pay taxes for benefits received. A bad reason for debt is to raise one generation's standard of living at the expense of a future generation. At best, this is an example of taxation without representation. At worst, it is stealing.

SO WHAT SHOULD I DO?

We were just kids playing in Alan's backyard, and somehow we got to talking about the future. It was then I learned that I didn't have one. Alan's older brother had it on good authority that the world was going to end in 1964. It would all come to a halt when the Russian menace launched its nuclear attack, and we were all going to be wiped out. I was worried.

I have vivid recollections of watching the TV with my folks, as a squat-faced, balding man beat the heel of his shoe on a podium and shouted angrily to Americans, *"We will bury you!"* That man was Nikita Khrushchev. He terrified me. If ever there was a man who could bring about the destruction of the world, he certainly appeared to me to be the one.

It's been many a year since I've thought about that man. He is no more today than the shadow of an unpleasant memory. But his name recently came up in conversation with my father. Dad was reflecting on how much he missed those precious hours of prayer when he and my mother, who is now with the Lord, would lay before the Lord their hopes, dreams, concerns, and longings. I'm not sure how it came up, but he told me that he and Mom would regularly pray for Khrushchev. He stood at the pinnacle of power in the Soviet Union and was in a position to do much harm or good. He was greatly in need of prayer. Dad went on to relate how he and Mom thought what a blessing it would be if, somehow, that man Khrushchev could come to accept for himself the truth of Christianity.

In America today, there are at least three ways we can influence government. First, we can become well informed and vote for representatives that best represent our values and beliefs. Second, we can choose to become personally involved as direct agents of government, by being elected to public office, accepting appointments, or serving vocationally with a government agency.

The third way could possibly be the most powerful instrument we have for influencing government. That is the way of prayer.

> I urge, then, first of all, that requests, prayers, intercession and thanksgiving be made for everyone—for kings and all those in authority, that we may live peaceful and quiet lives in all godliness and holiness. This is good, and pleases God our Savior. (1 Timothy 2:1-3)

I confess that I do not pray enough. But I do pray more than I did last year and even more than the year before. I want to constantly grow in this dimension of life. I ask myself, if our president had to rely on *my prayers* to supply him with the wisdom and courage that is needed to serve the land, how well would he be supplied?

My parents did not need to agree with Nikita Khrushchev to bathe him in prayer. Actually, the fact that they disagreed with virtually everything he stood for made it all the more urgent that they pray. In my own prayers, I ask that God would strongly support any action that our government takes that is consistent with the desires of God and that he would oppose and confuse any course of action that is contrary to the way of truth. In this way I can pray honestly. If Christianity is to carry the day in a pluralistic democracy, it will be a process that begins on our knees.

CHAPTER 7

Getting a Grip on Your Finances

Personal economic planning

ONE GOAL of this book is to help us focus on what is right in our economy today and how, as Christians, we can relate to economic issues. Even though I may have painted a positive picture of the economy as a whole, the fact is that many people would point to their own personal financial situation as a real pressure point in their life. Some have singled out credit as the principal villain. I'll agree that the use of credit is an important issue, but I think the real danger has more to do with old-fashioned greed than it does with credit.

Greed is one of those words that gets used frequently in a variety of contexts. Overuse of a word can dilute its meaning. I decided to look up the word *greed* in the dictionary. I found that it means "excessive or reprehensible acquisitiveness."[1] I then looked up *acquisitive*, which is defined as "strongly desirous of acquiring and possessing."[2]

Greed is not so much a material state but rather an attitude. We are greedy when we always want more. The fact that greed is an attitude means it is possible for anyone to be greedy. Whether you have a lot or a little, you may always want more. Credit can become the vehicle for fueling our greed.

Because greed is an attitude, it is a problem of the heart. At its root is a lack of contentment with the provision of God. Unlike the apostle Paul, we have not become good at being content in whatever state we find ourselves.

Unfortunately, we are encouraged in many ways to use credit to increase our present consumption. *Want it? Charge it! Dispel your boredom and master the possibilities with MasterCard. Enter a new world of discovery with Discover.* We organize our patterns of spending around the one "low" monthly payment. But the payments add up, and people end up working two jobs, having hectic schedules, being unhappy about quality and quantity of family time, being unable to help meet true financial needs of others, and feeling generally stressed out. And this is what they call the good life.

To be financially successful is to be free of acute stress in this area of our lives. We have a grip on it and not the other way around.

★ ★ ★ ★ ★

There is a better way. There is a way to be personally financially successful. To be financially successful is to be free of acute stress in this area of our lives. We have a grip on it and not the other way around. Success is not measured by your income or the amount of money you have. I define it this way: You are financially successful when, on a list of the stressors in your life, money issues are low on the list or fail to appear at all. To be sure, they will be there from time to time, but when financial matters and problems consistently dominate your life, something is not working right.

There is a way to become financially successful. It is simple but not easy.

First you give.

Next you save.

Then you live on what is left.

It really is just that simple—and just that difficult.

FIRST YOU GIVE

Ever since I was a young child, tithing was just something that our family did as a starting point for giving. Every week, my dad gave me five nickels for my allowance. I had my church offering envelopes with three boxes. One was for the building fund, another was for missions, and the third was for the current fund. My dad showed me that I could take three of those nickels each week and designate one nickel for each box. That would leave me one nickel to save and one to spend. So each week, I'd put my three nickels in the envelope and designate five cents for the building fund and ten cents for the missionaries. I'd generally ignore the other box because I wasn't sure what "current" was in the first place, and whatever it was, I was highly dubious that the church needed to buy any more of it.

You don't have to be a math whiz to figure out that I was giving up 60 percent of my allowance each week, saving 20 percent, and spending 20 percent. Coming from that perspective, I was pleased as punch when, later in life, I learned about tithing—giving 10 percent—as a starting point for giving. My wife's situation growing up was similar to mine. As a result, we've developed the habit of giving without ever having to really decide to do so. Most other people have not been so fortunate. As a result, the matter of giving can appear to present quite a formidable challenge.

As a certified public accountant and a professor in business, I have worked with a wide range of people on matters relating to their personal finances. I have never met anyone who practiced tithing who also pointed to their personal financial situation as a major point of stress. It didn't matter whether they were wealthy or had very modest means. If they were givers, they were free from financial stress. On the other hand, I have worked with some people who made a great deal of money and still suffered from significant stress related to their personal financial situation. They were not givers.

In Malachi 3:8-10 we read,

> "Will a man rob God? Yet you rob me. But you ask, 'How do we rob you?' In tithes and offerings. You are under a curse—the whole nation of you—because you are robbing me. Bring the whole tithe into the storehouse, that there may be food in my house. Test me in this," says the Lord Almighty, "and see if I will not throw open the floodgates of heaven and pour out so much blessing that you will not have room enough for it."

Just what is the nature of this blessing? It does not mean that you will become rich by this world's standards. Unfortunately the airwaves are full of misguided—if not outright deceitful—people who call upon us to give $100 to their "ministry" and receive back tenfold as much from the hand of God. Such claims are not supported by Scripture. But God does promise us his blessing. I believe it is the blessing of contentment. It is this contentment that Paul speaks about when writing to Timothy:

> Godliness *with contentment* is great gain. For we brought nothing into the world, and we can take noth-

ing out of it. But if we have food and clothing, we will be content with that. (1 Timothy 6:6-8, emphasis added)

Leviticus 27:30-32 says a tenth is the Lord's and it is holy. Numbers 18:28-29 tells us the best of the tithe is the Lord's. Proverbs 3:9 says to "Honor the Lord with your wealth, with the firstfruits of all your crops." In Matthew 23:23 Jesus teaches us not to ignore matters of justice and not to neglect the tithe. First Corinthians 16:2 teaches consistent, regular giving out of our abundance.

That we are to give is clear. I encourage you to study the entire breadth of Scripture on the matter. I have done so and concluded that, as a minimum, one-tenth of our family's gross income is to be directed to the Lord's work. And to the extent that we prosper, we give offerings beyond the tithe, out of our abundance.

> *One-tenth of our family's gross income is to be directed to the Lord's work. And to the extent that we prosper, we give offerings beyond the tithe, out of our abundance.*
>
> ★ ★ ★ ★ ★

The tithe in the Old Testament was designated to maintain the ministry of the Levites, who ministered on behalf of the people of Israel.

> I give to the Levites all the tithes in Israel as their inheritance in return for the work they do while serving at the Tent of Meeting. (Numbers 18:21)

The Levites were the only tribe that didn't receive a section of the Promised Land. To be without land in that society was to be virtually without means of support. If the people with land did not share their produce with the Levites, ministry would have ceased. We have a parallel situation today with people who minister on behalf of the church. Many have no other source of income, and the various ministries of the church depend on the tithes and offerings of God's people.

In Deuteronomy 14:22-29, Scripture teaches about a second tithe that was designated for personal worship and celebration of the blessings of God. Every third year, this tithe was to go to the poor.

In one sense, it seems somewhat futile to speak about the tithe when the current practice of the church at large is nowhere near a 10-percent level of giving. One study of thirty-one Protestant denominations showed that in 1990, people gave only 2.6 percent of their after-tax income to churches.[3] People making less than $10,000 a year give the most to their churches and other charities, according to a survey conducted for Washington-based Independent Sector. People making incomes of $50,000 to $75,000 were reported to give only 1.5 percent.[4]

The principal reason that I stress giving as the starting point for financial contentment is that I firmly believe that our hearts will follow our treasure. Show me how you spend your money, and I'll tell you what's most important in your life. When our treasure flows to the Lord's work, it is his work that becomes important to us. Have you ever invested in stocks? Afterwards, you probably checked the daily quotations in the newspaper to see how well your investment was doing. The same thing will be true when you enter into a commitment to support a missionary. When your treasure flows to Ecuador, you read the newspaper more carefully when it touches on Latin America. In a similar way, your thoughts, concerns, interests, prayers, and heart can be drawn to your church, the inner city, or Africa as you commit your treasure to the work of the Lord.

Getting a grip on your finances all begins with getting your priorities straight. If your treasure each month is devoted to meeting the payments on that beautiful car sitting out in the driveway, then there's a better-than-even chance that is where your heart is going to go. The importance of *things* can crowd out the importance of what matters most to God. That is a formula for discontentment and frustration with one's personal financial situation.

The principal reason that I stress giving as the starting point for financial contentment is that I firmly believe that our hearts will follow our treasure. Show me how you spend your money, and I'll tell you what's most important in your life.

★ ★ ★ ★ ★

NEXT YOU SAVE

While the Bible has a great deal to say about giving, I do not find that the Bible speaks directly to the issue of saving. There are only some indirect references.

Proverbs 6:6-8 gives the example of the ant, which stores its provisions in the summer and gathers its food at harvest. This proverb commends both the forward-looking nature and industry of the ant. Proverbs 13:22 says, "A good man leaves an inheritance for his children's children, but a sinner's wealth is stored up for the righteous." This verse is sometimes used as justification for building a financial estate for one's heirs, but it doesn't appear that this is the main thrust of the teaching.

The best scriptural support for developing a consistent plan of savings can be found, I believe, in 1 Timothy 5:8, where Christians are commanded to provide for their families: "If anyone does not provide for his relatives, and especially for his immediate family, he has denied the faith and is worse than an unbeliever."

Establishing a habit of saving is one tangible way that we can provide for our families in the event that we lose our job, become disabled, or otherwise lose our source of current income. I know of several situations where men have had to quit their job because they felt they were being called upon to act in unethical ways. They could do so, giving up a current flow of income, and still provide for the needs of their family because a well-developed habit of saving in the past provided the means to meet current needs.

This is also a way that parents can help children avoid assuming heavy burdens of debt to finance a college education. It can provide the means to help young families break into the housing market. In the event of the death of a spouse, it can also provide for the family at a critical point in time. To have the stress of losing a spouse compounded by the added pressure of not knowing how to provide for the family is more than anyone should have to bear.

One of the fringe benefits of saving regularly is that it teaches you how to say no to things and not spend everything you earn. You are, in fact, learning self-discipline with respect to managing your money. Developing discipline in any area of your life just makes it that much easier to exercise discipline in other areas.

When it comes to savings, it pays to start young. If you were to start a savings plan at age 25, saving $1,000 a year every year in an account that earned 8 percent compounded annually, at age 65 you would have accumulated a total of $259,065. You would have watched a $1,000 annual investment, totalling $40,000, grow to over a quarter of a million dollars in forty years. If, however, you waited until age 35 to begin saving $1,000 each year, that $30,000 total investment would only grow to $113,283 at age 65. Trading future savings for $1,000 of additional spending every year from age 25 to 34 would cost you almost $140,000 at retirement. But even starting at 35 is better than waiting until you're 45. Waiting another ten years, then saving $1,000 a year from age 45 to 65, would amount to only $45,762 at age 65. Remember, you would have $113,282 if you had begun at age 35. Waiting those ten years means trading $10,000 in current spending for $65,521 at retirement. Because of the nature of compounding interest, the penalty for waiting to start saving is severe.

RESULTS OF $1,000/YEAR INVESTMENT AT 8% INTEREST

Age you started saving	25	35	45
Total investment by age 65	$40,000	$30,000	$20,000
Value of your investment, plus interest, at age 65	$259,065	$113,283	$45,762

If you haven't begun a savings plan yet, these numbers may be a bit discouraging to you. But if you have been part of a pension, profit-sharing, or some other retirement program with your employer, this arithmetic will still be working for you. What may seem to be small contributions to a retirement program, made during the early years of a career, can compound themselves into significant benefits at retirement.

You may feel, given the current state of your finances, that you just can't possibly begin a savings plan right now. In that case, I'd still encourage you to develop the habit by saving nickels, dimes, or quarters each week. It may not be much, but it will be the start of a good habit that can grow as your finances become more under control.

An important implication of becoming

An important implication of becoming a saver is that you will have to begin to learn something about investing.

★ ★ ★ ★ ★

a saver is that you will have to begin to learn something about investing. Many people have questions about what makes for a wise investment. I have a few principles to suggest.

A person once came to me and asked my opinion about where she should invest her money if she was interested in a certificate of deposit. I recommended a few good options. She came back later and showed me a comparison of interest rates that she could earn on CD's from different institutions. Some out-of-state institutions were offering rates that were significantly higher than places that I had suggested. Showing me a newspaper ad, she wondered why I hadn't recommended some of the higher-paying CD's.

There was a reason why those institutions had to go out of state to raise money and offer rates that were extraordinary by normal standards. The reason was that locals who knew what was going on wouldn't invest a dime with those institutions. They were high-risk investments that could only attract new money by offering unusually high rates of return. The question was, would they be in a position to pay up? As it turned out, they were not. They folded.

When it comes to investing, the wisest investment is not always the one that offers the highest potential rewards. There is a trade-off between risk and reward. Higher rewards generally come at the expense of assuming higher risk. When deciding on investments, you should first decide on how much risk you are willing to assume. Then you can shop around for the best opportunities for return within a given class of risk.

There are different types of risk associated with investments. The possibility of default or bankruptcy is one source of risk. Long-term investments are riskier than short-term investments. One obvious reason is that there is a greater chance that things can go wrong with either the company, the industry, the economy, or the world in general. The longer the term of the investment, the greater chance there is that business conditions could change and impair the security of your investment. But there is another less obvious risk associated with long-term, fixed-return investments such as bonds. The longer the investment, the more sensitive it is to changes in interest rates. To see how this might be so, assume you purchased a bond that offered a 7 percent fixed return at the time of your initial investment. Its market value would deteriorate if interest rates in the general marketplace rose above 7 percent. Because buyers would insist on earning the higher market return and could only achieve that by purchasing your investment at a discount, you would most certainly lose some of the original principal, in the event you had to sell off that particular bond. This problem is more severe with long-term than with short-term bonds.

The safest investments are short-term treasury bills of the United States Government. As we saw in chapter 1, there is no reason for concern about investing in our government or its banks. U.S. Treasury bills are considered by the financial world to be virtually free from risk of default. Treasury bills (also called T-bills) are, in effect, short-term loans made to the U.S. government that are repaid in one year or less. Other low-risk investments are insured savings deposits at banks and savings and loans. You should ask to make sure the bank is indeed insured and also what the limits of the coverage are.

Bonds are generally considered to be less risky than stocks. When you buy a bond, you are really lending money to the issuer of the bond—usually a large corporation, a government unit, or government agency—who then uses the money to finance some long-term project. The bond issuer (the borrower) promises to pay you interest, generally twice a year, and also promises to repay the principal amount of the bond at the end of the loan, possibly as many as five to twenty years down the road. The Disney Corporation issued bonds in 1993 that it will not repay until the year 2093, one hundred years later. Obviously, the security of a bond depends on which corporation or government unit is doing the borrowing. Many bonds are considered to be low-risk investments because of the high-quality credit rating of the borrower. In cases where there is great uncertainty about the financial strength of the bond issuer, the bond could in fact be a very speculative type of investment. Junk bonds would fall into this category.

All bonds, however, can suffer relatively large swings in market value when interest rates move. The value of bonds moves inversely with the movements in interest rates. When interest rates move up, bond prices fall, and vice versa. But because bonds make a legal commitment to repay principal and to pay interest at prescribed points in time, and because payments to bondholders take precedence over payments to shareholders, bonds are thought to bear less risk than common stocks.

Stocks, like some bonds, are issued by corporations. But unlike bonds, stocks are not guaranteed to pay interest. Nor does the corporation promise to return the original investment amount. When you buy a stock, you are becoming part owner of the business rather than a lender, as when you buy a bond. While stocks do not pay interest, most do pay dividends on a regular basis. These dividends are really a distribution of corporations' profits to the shareholders (owners).

Stocks are riskier than bonds. Not only do stock prices

behave in a volatile fashion, there is no guarantee that the company will pay its dividend. The only way to get your principal investment returned is to sell your stock.

Looking back over the last forty years or more, we see that common stocks have provided the highest long-term return on investment. But stocks have historically been a volatile investment, with values increasing or decreasing dramatically over short periods of time. If you are investing for the long haul, five years or more, then common stocks are a good choice. But if it is likely that you might need to liquidate your investment in the next few years, then it's probably a good idea to settle for investments that offer less potential return but carry less risk of losing your principal investment.

When you are investing, it is impossible to avoid risk. But it is important to understand the level of risk you are assuming. As a general rule, I recommend that people never invest in anything that they don't understand. If you are unfamiliar with the world of investments and are looking for a user-friendly way to introduce yourself to the different kinds of in-

> *I recommend that people never invest in anything that they don't understand.*
>
> ★ ★ ★ ★ ★

vestment instruments that are out there, I recommend that you pick up *The Wall Street Journal Guide to Understanding Money and Investing* by Kenneth M. Morris and Alan M. Siegel (Lightbulb Press, 1993).

Because the world of investments is complicated and changing rapidly, I recommend that people seek out competent investment counsel. You will know if you are dealing with someone who is competent if they can help you understand the type and degree of risk associated with an investment they may be recommending. If the experts cannot explain something to the extent that you are able to understand it, then it is virtually certain that they don't really understand what they are recommending.

I also firmly believe that one spouse should never invest in anything that cannot be explained to the other spouse. I would again apply the same standard: If you can't explain something to your husband or wife in a way that makes sense, then you don't understand it well enough yourself. Before any of a family's savings are invested, I firmly recommend that both husband and wife come to full agreement. Risk is something that both spouses must bear. There are simply too many sad stories where the family savings have been unknowingly frittered away from losses on risky investments made by either a husband or wife without the knowledge or consent of a spouse.

Then You Live on What's Left

Some people find that living on what's left is oppressive. This may be true for families where the breadwinners have suddenly found themselves unemployed or disabled with their source of income cut off or greatly diminished. There are also people who, for a variety of reasons, are destitute and living in poverty. For these people, living on what is left is a story of human tragedy. This is not the situation I am addressing. I intend to address that segment of our society who, like me, make enough to live on but struggle with the "too much month at the end of the money" syndrome. We can become oppressed in spirit by the task of making ends meet.

Let me encourage you to rethink this particular dimension of life. Living on what is left can be very fulfilling and even fun. Ruthie and I agree that life keeps getting better, but we still look back on our early years of marriage with fond memories. During the first three years we were married, one or the other of us was a full-time student at any given time. Money was scarce in those days, but learning to meet this challenge together was a terrific way to grow in our marriage. We lived on the second story of a house, with our landlords on the first floor. Our apartment was furnished with a combination of hand-me-downs and garage-sale specials. Our couch cost the princely sum of fifteen dollars. Our end tables were orange crates that we painted.

My occupation of teaching in a Christian college has continued to provide our family with financial challenges over the years. Meeting these challenges continues to do good things for our family. Several years ago, my daughter, Lisa, developed a desire for a new bicycle. She had truly outgrown her "baby bike," and it was time for another. She wanted it to be pink, have a saddle seat, and a pretty basket on the front. Unfortunately, she developed this longing at a time when the monthly cash flow was already getting squeezed. I explained this to her and asked her how she would feel about looking for a nice bike at a garage sale the next Saturday. She wasn't delighted at the prospect, but she was willing to give it a try. She understood that money was tight and we really needed to be careful.

The night before we were to go looking for this bike, Lisa did something novel. In our bedtime prayers she suggested that we bring the matter before the Lord. It is moments like this when life butts up against my own faith like a bully on the playground. Does God really care about these things?

I let *her* pray that night.

The next morning we got in the car and headed off in our quest for the perfect bike. We had traveled about five minutes when all of a sudden Lisa yelled, *"Stop, Daddy!"*

I did as I was told. I pulled up alongside the curb in front of a nice home, and there in the driveway were not one, but *two* shiny girl's bikes for sale. They were just the right size. They were pink . . . had saddle seats . . . and pretty wicker baskets on the front . . . with flowers on the baskets.

The family at this house had lovely little twin girls. The bikes had been a present to them, and they had quickly outgrown them. They were virtually brand-new. Lisa picked one; I paid twenty dollars, got into the car, and marvelled at the fact that God cared about my little girl's bike.

Lisa's response? "Gee, Dad, I didn't even ask God for the flowers, but I really love them!"

God also cares about plumbing. I had just finished washing dishes at the sink and was letting the water drain out when I heard that telltale sound of *glub-glub-glub* from deep within the drain. It bubbled and burped once or twice and that was it. The drain was stopped up. I plunged and probed the drain from the sink side to no avail. This problem required a trip to the crawl space below the kitchen floor. It had to be attacked from the trap below. The only problem with this strategy was that the trap had not been opened in over twenty years. Even with the best of my efforts, it appeared that it would remain sealed tight for the next twenty years.

I won't bore you with the details of the few hours that I spent trying to open that trap. Suffice it to say that I experienced the entire gamut of emotions that come with fruitless efforts expended under unpleasant, if not downright hostile, physical circumstances. There I was, lying on my back in that crawl space, tired, winded, and frustrated. I was just staring at that stupid pipe when I got the idea,

Hey! Why don't you just pray about the pipe?

"What?" I replied to myself.

Pray about it; just go ahead and pray about it.

It took me several moments of further reflection about this conversation I was having with myself before I decided to give it a try. My prayer went something like this:

"Lord, you know that we try to take the money you provide our family and use it wisely. Now, Lord, I'm willing to give this pipe one last try. But if I can't get it open, I am going to take some of *your* money and give it to a plumber. I am perfectly willing to do that, but if you would rather I not, then you'll have to help me get this cap loose. Amen."

It was not a very eloquent prayer. Neither was it emotional. It was a matter-of-fact type of prayer, simply relating to God what I was thinking at the time. I laid there a moment or two longer, staring at that configuration of pipe, and it dawned on me that there was a new angle from which to apply pressure to the cap that I hadn't yet tried. (I hadn't seen this angle before because it required the perspective that came from lying on my back beneath the pipe.) With renewed interest I clamped the pipe wrench to the cap, braced my feet against the floor joists above, and was able to use my legs as well as my upper body strength to pull against that pipe. There I hung, like a bat upside down, pulling for all I was worth, and I felt it give! It was only a little movement, but it was real. My further efforts were duly rewarded, and the cap came loose. Would you understand me if I said it was almost a holy moment? God cared about my plumbing.

We don't buy everything used. Neither do we frequently go to garage sales. I do, in fact, sometimes require the services of a plumber. He knows our house only too well. The point that I am trying to make is that learning to live on what is left almost always requires God's help. As you learn to live on what's left, you are learning to lean on God. That's what he wants. That is also what is best for us.

SO WHAT SHOULD I DO?

First you give, next you save, and then you live on what's left. Easy to say. Much harder to do. Living on what is left, for most of us, requires an understanding of the relationship between our income and our living expenses. A budget is very helpful in sorting this out. There are a variety of ways to approach the budget process.

> **Learning to live on what is left almost always requires God's help. As you learn to live on what's left, you are learning to lean on God.**
>
> ★ ★ ★ ★ ★

I know one couple who uses Monopoly money to represent the monthly paycheck. Each month they "cash" the family paycheck into Monopoly money, which they put into various envelopes designated for food, utilities, gifts, entertainment, housing payments, saving, tithing, and other expenses they expect that month. When they write checks or spend actual money throughout the month, they then remove the play money from the appropriate envelope. When the play money is gone, it is a visual and physical reminder that they cannot afford to spend any more.

Admittedly, this may be a bit extreme for many people, but it works great for this young couple. There are a host of good personal money management books out there that can help you set a budget. If you feel like your finances are out of control, I recommend that you begin the process of getting a grip on them by investing in one of these good books. I have found the writings of Ron Blue to be very practical and balanced in this area. Two fine books are *The Christian's Guide to Worry-free Money Management* by Daniel

Busby, Kent Barber, and Robert Temple, and *Does God Care if I Can't Pay My Bills?* by Linda K. Taylor.

If you are married, I have a couple of practical pointers for making the financial dimension of your life go more smoothly. When two people get married, Scripture says that the two become one. It is dangerous to enter marriage with a "yours" and "mine" mentality about money. Paychecks, whether earned by husband or wife, should go into a common fund from which the family can meet its needs. I would argue that separate checking accounts are problematic. Remember, your heart will follow your money. If you cannot trust your spouse with the family finances, that is a sign of a lack of commitment. For marriage to work, it must begin with mutual respect and commitment.

> *Paychecks, whether earned by husband or wife, should go to a common fund from which the family can meet its needs.*
>
> ★ ★ ★ ★ ★

When it comes to spending money, I believe that both husband and wife should agree on a purchase before any significant amount of money is spent. In our family, my wife and I each have veto power when it comes to spending money. If I believe we "need" something and Ruthie does not, then we don't buy it. People often want to know what dollar amount you should use as the point where you need to first check with your spouse before spending. It will vary from household to household, but I do know this: When you violate the principle, you'll find out.

It doesn't always work out smoothly in our family. In fact, implementing this principle has provided Ruthie and me with some of our best opportunities to develop conflict-resolution skills. Allow me to share with you one such opportunity we had.

We were anticipating the birth of our third child, and as you might expect, we were giving some thought to preparing the "baby's room." Actually, Ruthie was giving it a great deal more thought than I was. I mostly supplied some muscle and elbow grease to help with the painting and wallpapering. In her musings on the matter, it occurred to Ruthie that the bedroom needed new carpet. When she mentioned this to me, I have to admit it was something of a revelation. I'd never noticed that the existing carpet was all that bad. Well, we went upstairs together to investigate the situation in light of this revelation. I looked down and saw carpet in a reasonably good state of repair. Ruthie looked down and saw ugly gold shag, a veritable eyesore. Furthermore, because it was so old it was likely harboring all sorts of micro-nasties that would be a definite menace to the health of a newborn child. She concluded that it had to go.

I was not phased by the color argument, but as a responsible father, I was forced to consider the health issue. I was in a bind on that one. Ruthie is the nurse in our family, and I have to defer to her on the health issues. All right, the carpet had to go. But underneath the carpet we had a beautiful hardwood floor that was no doubt in superb condition, since it had always been covered with carpet. Better yet, I argued, a hardwood floor couldn't possibly harbor germs like a carpet could. That was the answer! We would get rid of the carpet and enjoy the beauty and sterility of the natural wood floor.

I was feeling quite satisfied with myself at that moment. I had discovered a way to deal with the issues of both appearance and health and hang on to some money as well. Ruthie was not feeling quite so satisfied with my conclusion. In her mind, we *definitely* needed new carpet in the room. But I carefully reiterated my position, and that ended the discussion. At least that's what I thought. Later that weekend, I was walking out the backdoor on my way to play tennis with my friend Chuck. Chuck was a very good tennis player. In fact, I had never beaten him in all the years we had been playing together.

As I was opening the door, Ruthie breezed by, wished me luck, and said, "Oh, by the way, honey, I'm going to run down to the store and pick up some carpet samples for the baby's room."

I closed the door. Puzzled, I said, "We're not getting new carpet for that room." I thought the issue had been clearly settled. I was confused, because I knew that in our household we didn't make this kind of expenditure unless we both agreed, and I knew that I had not agreed to it.

Ruthie, on the other hand, had interpreted my silence as assent—or at least acquiescence—and was proceeding full steam ahead. When you're moving ahead with full force on something, it's pretty unpleasant to come to an abrupt halt. It's especially unpleasant when the one putting on the brakes is your husband, standing there with a dumb look on his face.

Upset isn't really the right word to describe how Ruthie felt. I'm not sure I should put the right words down in print. Suffice it to say that she turned on her heel and stormed out of the room.

I found these last few moments to be quite bizarre. I hadn't seen this coming, and I really didn't know what to make of it. But I did know I was going to be late for my tennis match, and I didn't have time to wait around for Ruthie to kiss me and say good-bye. So I left.

As I was pulling out of the driveway, Ruthie appeared at the front door of the house. She threw open the door and shouted at me, "DON'T YOU EVER LEAVE THIS HOUSE WITHOUT SAYING GOOD-BYE TO ME AGAIN!" With that, she slammed the door.

For the first time in my life, I beat Chuck at tennis. In fact, I trounced him. He's still wondering what got into me that afternoon.

By the way, the new carpet was baby blue.

Please don't conclude from this episode that working as a team on the family finances is the wrong way to go. It is the *only* way to go. Realistically, the going can sometimes get a little bumpy, but the ride is definitely worth it.

> **The management of any family's finances will be better when husband and wife share in the process and work as a team.**
> ★ ★ ★ ★ ★

Working as a team not only requires mutual agreement on any significant expenditure, it also means mutual involvement in things like paying the bills. I suggest that spouses share this responsibility. One can do it one year, the other can do it the next. This has several benefits. It gives both husband and wife a good sense of what things cost and what the family can or cannot afford. This makes achieving consensus easier. It is also a fact of life that one spouse will most likely outlive the other. That situation provides sufficient stress in and of itself. When you add to that the task of having to manage the family finances, it can be overwhelming if you have never before had a meaningful role in administering them.

The best reason for working as a team is that you will find your spouse has wonderful insights and can bring wise counsel on the financial matters that face your family. I am a certified public accountant. I have a master's degree in business. I have a Ph.D. in economics. I have worked in finance, tax accounting, and administration for years. But I must say, the best financial moves for our family have been those initiated by my wife, who has worked as a mom and a nurse for the last twenty years. I am constantly amazed at her insights into what is and isn't good for our family. The best thing that I have contributed to the financial management of our family over the years is to learn to listen to Ruthie. I am convinced our situation is not unique. The management of any family's finances will be better when husband and wife share in the process and work as a team.

You don't have to be married to benefit from the counsel of others. A good friend will have your best interests at heart and will be concerned about your welfare. A good friend can also be honest with you. Figuring out what makes sense financially sometimes requires the caring and more objective analysis that a friend can offer. Go ahead and take advantage of it.

I would like to offer two last suggestions. I have noticed that sometimes, people can adopt a "penny-wise, dollar-foolish" mentality to managing finances. I think men are particularly prone to this, but it will also appear among women.

A young mom once came home from a shopping trip with her three small children all decked out in new gym shoes. Like popcorn popping, the kids proudly bounced up to Dad, eager to show him their recent purchases. He looked down and saw ninety bucks bouncing around the room and wasn't happy about it. It was actually worse than it first appeared—because in walked Mom with three boxes of Sunday shoes as well. He didn't have to say a thing. The kids knew that Dad was mad. The balloon was burst and the joy of the moment hissed out of the room. Three little kids melted out of sight.

Later that week, the same dad came bouncing home one afternoon with a great surprise for his wife.

"Honey, come outside. I want you to see something. It's a surprise!"

Outside sat a new car . . . "their" new car.

Well, you can draw your own conclusions. Shoes are expensive. Cars are more expensive.

I too can be guilty of this penny-wise, dollar-foolish mentality. For several years around Christmastime, Ruthie and I would go out for a special dinner with three other couples who were some of our closest friends. It was always a special time, and we enjoyed it immensely. One year the four wives decided we should go to a Japanese restaurant in downtown Chicago, about thirty miles from where we all lived. Ruthie and I had been there once before, though, and while the food was excellent and the atmosphere engaging, I concluded it was a bit pricey for what you got.

When Ruthie told me about the plans, in my mind I quickly calculated: baby-sitter $15, parking $10, dinner $60. I was looking at an $85 evening. Being prone to fits of personal piety at moments such as this, I convinced myself that this was bad stewardship of our family's resources, and so I suggested to Ruthie that we take a pass on this one.

When that evening came, the other three couples got all gussied up in their holiday best and went off into the cold night to share the warmth of an evening together with friends around delicious food.

We stayed home alone and had SpaghettiOs. And if it was cold that night in Chicago, it was downright frigid in our house.

When it comes to making financial choices for our family, I believe that was as bad a mistake as I have ever made. I was younger then, and I wasn't exactly sure what I had done wrong. I now understand that while I looked at the situation and concluded that $85 was too much to spend on dinner, Ruthie looked at the same situation and concluded that I didn't think *she* was worth $85. It wasn't about dinner, it was about spending a special evening with my wife.

Men, when it comes to spending money on your wife, sometimes it pays to be "extravagant." Whatever it is you're buying will seldom be worth it in your eyes, but believe me, your wife is worth it. I'm sure the same principle applies to parents, children, and anyone who is special in your life.

One last caution, guys, when it comes to buying presents for your wife, I have learned this lesson: If you can plug it in, it's not a gift. We men value the concept of combining electricity with gifts. This translates into power tools, video and audio equipment, and various other man-toys. For most women, however, a toaster on Mother's Day doesn't cut it. In my own gift-buying pilgrimage, I have had to do some growing. I have even learned to shop for the "L-word"—*lingerie.* This represents the ultimate "lay it on the line for your wife" type of gift.

When it comes to buying presents for your wife, I have learned this lesson: If you can plug it in, it's not a gift.

★ ★ ★ ★ ★

I still haven't learned to do it without wearing a paper bag over my head, though. The one time I tried it without my bag, I was waited on by one of my former students. When she came up to ask if she could help me, I immediately recognized her, and with my face turning every possible shade of red, I muttered something like, "Uh, well . . . yes, you can . . . sure . . . uh, uh . . . can you show me where I can find a pipe wrench?"

She responded, "Why don't you try our hardware department?"

"Now, that's a good idea. Why didn't I think of that? Thanks ever so much!"

Yes, indeed, making financial choices for the family does have its challenges. But there is every reason to be optimistic about this area of our lives. God wishes us to have success in managing our family finances. I'd again encourage you to think about following this formula:

First you give. Next you save. Then you live on what's left. It is as simple, and as hard, as that.

CHAPTER 8

What Is It Worth?

The defining question of economics

NOT TOO FAR from where we live there is one of those super amusement theme parks. I have never been there myself, but my kids have gone a few times with groups from school or church. The last time my son went, I gave him ten bucks as food money for the day. His group left on a bus early that morning, and they did not return until late in the evening. My son came home and went straight to the refrigerator. He chowed down food and guzzled various beverages as if he hadn't had a thing to eat or drink all day.

This turned out to be exactly the case. It had been a long, hot summer day, but he had not spent any of the money I had given him for food. I was amazed.

"Why on earth didn't you get something to eat or drink at the park?" I asked.

My son responded that he was so disgusted with the exorbitant prices that were being charged for concessions that he decided he wasn't going to succumb to such a gross economic injustice. He wasn't going to be cheated. I resisted the impulse that comes from being an economics professor to use the moment to instruct him on the workings of a local monopoly. I just kept my mouth shut and tried to listen like a good father.

The theme park is, after all, a business. They didn't coerce my son into coming to the park. Nor did they force him to trade his ten dollars for food. They had placed a value on their food and drink, and my son didn't agree with their assessment. It was my son's choice to refuse to pay their prices. And yet he felt violated by the situation.

In economics, a foundational principle is that of *economic value*. Define economic value, and you will touch the principles of exchange, wages, profits, trade, choice, individualism, community, justice, economic self-determination, political organization, tariffs, taxes, welfare, and a host of other economic issues.

Consider just one implication, that of price. Prices ought to be the measure of the worth of something. What is it worth? An easy question, right? A question people unconsciously answer and act on every day in countless ways, without ever really giving much consideration to the underlying question of what determines value in the first place. Every time a person makes a purchasing choice, that individual is making either conscious or subconscious evaluations of the worth of each alternative option. As pointed out by Edwin Cannan, on those rare occasions when a person does stop to consider the idea of value, it is generally done in the context of some perceived injustice with respect to the price of a commodity or service.[1]

This, in fact, is what happened when my son went to the amusement park. But we have all had similar experiences. Have you ever thought a repair bill was inflated? Did you ever pay "too much" for gas on the interstate? Have you ever been "overcharged" for a cab ride from the airport? Have you ever thought the price of a new car was simply absurd?

The bill comes from the hospital. "That's *outrageous!*" you say—but how do you know? The point is that we do have a definite tendency to look at a given price and conclude, "That's too much!" We have experienced these situations personally and know that they are often very emotionally charged. But having strong "feelings" that a price is wrong does not necessarily help us figure out what the right price is; and that's our problem. That is why we have to come to an understanding of the nature of value. Defining the nature of value is the first step in the process of arriving at the "right price."

Have you ever thought a repair bill was inflated? Did you ever pay "too much" for gas on the interstate? Have you ever been "overcharged" for a cab ride from the airport?

★ ★ ★ ★ ★

The earliest formal considerations of economic value tended to focus on the ethical considerations of price. It wasn't until the seventeenth century that moral philosophers tended to shift the focus of the discussion to economic rather than ethical considerations of the notion of value as manifested in prices.

The definitions of economic value can be categorized into three groups. I think of them as "inside" definitions, "outside" definitions, and finally "outside-inside" definitions. The "inside" group sees economic value as something that is innate *within* an object. Some would argue that the intrinsic value of a product or service can be determined by the amount of labor or cost embodied in it. What is it worth? Tell them how much work went into making it, and they'll tell you. Under this definition, value is intrinsic, absolute, not subject to variation.

In contrast to that position are the "outside" definitions, which hold that economic value is imputed to an object from the *outside,* by the consumer. There is inherently no value in anything unless someone believes it has value. There is no absolute measure of value. Value is relative and totally subjective.

Since I referred to the third group of definitions as an "outside-inside" approach, you may already have guessed that this approach incorporates elements of both previous perspectives. This view draws on generally accepted standards of fairness in dealing with questions of economic value. The thought is that all goods and services have an inherent (inside) price that reasonable people would consider to be a fair or "just" valuation of its worth. This "just price" acts the same as if it were embodied in the object itself, but it is really the result of a common (outside) valuation imputed to it by the general public.

WHO'S IN CHARGE?

Whether people realize it or not, they have already chosen one of these definitions of economic value as the proper way of looking at the world. That choice will, in turn, influence their decisions on how to organize the economy; that is, to what degree does the state need to be involved? Since the link between defining value and the involvement of government in the economic system is not always obvious, it is worth taking a moment to develop a good understanding of the definitions of economic value and how they relate to the issue of organizing the economy.

We will look first at two ideas of economic value that represent the inside group of definitions. Both the *labor* and *cost* theories of value are inside perspectives stemming from the belief that value is embodied within things and can be measured by the amount of either labor or cost that went into the production process. This view generally necessitates a large role for government and a small role for free markets. Economic activity tends to become directed by government rather than by markets.

The dominant outside theory of value embraces the notion of *utility*—a broad concept of usefulness that includes any quality that contributes to our general well-being. With this view, free markets play a key role in economic organization.

Finally, we will look at *just price* theories of economic value as an example of the outside-inside group of definitions. Government will play a large and significant part when economic activity is organized according to just price theories of value.

LABOR THEORY OF VALUE

It can hardly be disputed that labor is a value-creating activity. Some have concluded that it is the *only* value-creating activity. They would argue that labor should be the sole measure of economic value in any commodity or object that has been transformed from its natural state. The dignity and worth of human labor, as a part of the essence of our life on earth, is an idea that has found wide (although not complete) acceptance from a variety of perspectives throughout history. Consider the following quotations, for example:

> May the favor of the Lord our God rest upon us; establish the work of our hands for us—yes, establish the work of our hands.   —*attributed to Moses, c. 1400 B.C.*[2]

Whatever you do, work at it with all your heart, as
working for the Lord, not for men, since you know
that you will receive an inheritance from the Lord
as a reward. It is the Lord Christ you are serving.
—*Paul the apostle, c. A.D. 60*[3]

Man hath his daily work of body or mind
Appointed, which declares his dignity,
And the regard of Heaven on all his ways.
—*John Milton, 1667*[4]

A man is upon the Wing, when he is at the Work,
which God hath set him to do. . . . Be a master of
your trade; count it a Disgrace to be no Workman
. . . . Oh, let every Christian Walk with God, when he
Works at his Calling, and Act in his Occupation with
an Eye to God.
—*Cotton Mather, Puritan, 1701*[5]

There is a perennial nobleness, and even sacredness,
in Work. . . . All true Work is sacred; in all true Work,
were it but true hand labour, there is something of
divineness.   —*Thomas Carlyle, 1843*[6]

Labor is the very touchstone for man's self-realiza-
tion, the medium of creating the world of his desire.
—*Karl Marx, 1867*[7]

Since labor is considered the sole determinant of economic value, prices—as the measure of an object's worth—
must somehow reflect the value of labor embodied within
the object. As a practical matter, you must somehow objec-
tively measure the quantity of labor required to produce a

specific good in question. It also requires a much more subjective evaluation of the quality of the labor needed.

How will the economy be structured if labor is the measure of economic value? First of all, prices are determined by embodied labor, so the "marketplace" will be organized according to the idea of equality in exchange espoused by Aristotle, where items are traded in proportions reflecting equal amounts of labor.

This will most likely lead to a "command" or government-directed economy, as opposed to a "demand" or market-directed economy. This is true for philosophical as well as practical reasons. Philosophically, since it has already been decided that economic value does not depend upon people's wants, it makes little sense to rely on consumer-driven markets to determine what should be produced. People's subjective valuations have already been dismissed in the economic equation.

How will the economy be structured if labor is the measure of economic value?

★ ★ ★ ★ ★

A government-directed economy also becomes a practical necessity, since producers lack the information that would be provided by true market prices. As we discussed in chapter 6, true market prices based upon individuals' valuations of things indicate what society wants and needs. In the absence of such information, producers will not know what to make. Automobile manufacturers cannot, for instance, look at a high market price for minivans and conclude that they ought to be making more minivans. Responsibility for deciding what and how much to make will, by default or intent, fall into the hands of government.

Another reason that government will become directly

involved in the economy relates to the problem of measuring labor inputs to determine prices. It becomes necessary to establish centralized government offices, which will then dictate the appropriate ratios of exchange. The government decides, for example, how many bushels of corn are equivalent to a ton of steel. Although a system of exchange prices may be established, the underlying reality is that this is much more like a complicated system of regulated barter than trade driven by actual market prices.

Given the practical problems associated with a labor theory of value, how is it that anyone could reasonably wish to organize economic activity based on that principle? The answer lies in part from a confusion between the value of *people* and the value of *things*. It is good and proper to have a high value of people, made in the image of God. Likewise it is good to have a high view of the nature and inherent value of a man's work. But while it isn't proper to look at people as things, neither is it proper to value things as you would a person. Many an error in life comes from doing just that.

Karl Marx is probably the best-known proponent of the labor theory of value. The impact of his thinking and writing on the course of history attests to the importance of the question of economic value and the problems with the labor theory in particular. What Marx had right was his high view of man and his work. What he had wrong was his view of human labor—rather than human beings themselves—as the supreme measure of value in guiding economic activity. Thus his version of the labor theory of value was not only impractical but immoral as well. Other versions of the labor theory of value may not necessarily be immoral, but rather be simply unworkable.

COST THEORY OF VALUE

Like the labor theory of value, the cost theory focuses on the value of what goes into a product rather than the value of the product itself. But it differs from the labor theory in that it recognizes a range of value-creating activities other than labor. For instance, the assumption of risk may be viewed as a value-creating activity. The owners and anyone else who contributes financial capital to fund the enterprise may also be considered part of the value-creating process. The cost theory has also enjoyed widespread popularity:

> When the price of any commodity is neither more nor less than what is sufficient to pay the rent of the land, wages of the labour, and the profits of the stock employed in raising, preparing, and bringing it to market, according to their natural rates, the commodity is then sold for what may be called its natural price.
> —*Adam Smith*, The Wealth of Nations, *1776*

> Company price setters often rely heavily on cost-plus pricing formulas. . . . Cost-based pricing formulas in manufacturing firms are likely to be "full cost" formulas, in which full cost is defined as estimated or standard manufacturing costs. . . .
> —Handbook of Modern Accounting, *1983*[8]

> Many people feel that cost-plus pricing is fairer to both buyers and sellers. Sellers do not take advantage of buyers when the latter's demand becomes acute; yet the sellers earn a fair return on their investment.
> —*Philip Kotler*, Marketing Management, *1984*[9]

The managerial economist has discovered some
fundamental errors committed by business executives in setting price. Some of these are . . . the
tendency to emphasize cost considerations over
demand considerations. (Characterized by state-
ments such as "I don't know what the traffic will
bear, but we had better ask for $10 per unit to
cover our cost and normal margin.") This tendency
reaches its pinnacle in cost-plus pricing where
demand considerations are simply ignored. There
is a deadly attractiveness in the apparent precision
and hardness of cost estimates which leads them
to receive excessive attention.

—Handbook of Modern Marketing, *1986*[10]

What does an economy organized around the cost theory of economic value look like? The answer depends on
what is considered a legitimate cost. If owners or other
suppliers of capital are not viewed as value creators, then
the system reverts back to essentially a labor theory.
There is no need to have prices any higher than is needed
to cover the value of labor inputs, raw materials, and
wear on equipment.

An economic system designed around this limited concept of cost would, just as in the case of the labor theory,
move toward a government-directed, or at least highly
regulated, system of economic organization, with costs
(and therefore prices) being determined by the appropriate authorities. Considerations of prices based upon will-
ingness to pay would be ignored for philosophical
reasons. Again, knowing what societies need and want
becomes difficult without a system of want/need-based
prices. The natural vacuum thus created would likely be

filled by some centralized state planning and directing agency. The responsibility for fixing the socially legitimate ratios of exchange, based upon cost, would also probably fall to this agency.

Using either labor or cost as the basis for determining economic value is a very limiting concept. It fails to recognize the potential gains from trade. Trade is reduced to the act of exchanging things of equal value with no increase in the total welfare of society. But voluntary trade occurs when two parties intuitively understand that they can each make themselves better off by exchange. Each party would rather have what the other currently is holding. By exchanging, they give up something of lesser value for something of greater perceived value and as a result come out ahead. Economic systems organized along the lines of cost definitions of value slow down or inhibit this value-creating process.

Using either labor or cost as the basis for determining economic value is a very limiting concept. It fails to recognize the potential gains from trade.

★ ★ ★ ★ ★

UTILITY THEORY OF VALUE

Pick up any economic principles textbook today and go to the chapter on how people make choices. It will talk about people making choices that satisfy their needs and wants in a way that provides them the maximum possible amount of total satisfaction or utility given the constraints of their budgets. Go to the chapter on how markets work. In that chapter you will see explanations of demand curves (they draw them mostly as straight lines). They all slope down and to the right. The standard joke about how to answer any question in Economics 101 is to just say "supply and demand."

Economic value is determined not by labor, not by cost, but by *utility imputed* to a commodity or service by people. If economic value consists of value attached to things by people, then it follows that the economy ought to be organized on the basis of the free choices of people within that society. Assuming it is true—that people will make choices they believe will improve rather than worsen their well-being—then people will only buy things at a price they perceive is fair. This theory, too, has been widely accepted:

> I observed that value is nothing inherent in goods and that it is not a property of goods. . . . The *measure* of value is entirely subjective in nature, and for this reason a good can have great value to one economizing individual, little value to another, and no value at all to a third. . . . The value an economizing individual attributes to a good is equal to the importance of the particular satisfaction that depends on his command of the good.   —*Carl Menger, 1871*[11]

> The final question needed to come to grips with business purpose and business mission is: "What is value to the customer?" It may be the most important question. . . . The customer never buys a product. By definition the customer buys the satisfaction of a want.   —*Peter Drucker, 1973*[12]

> An increasing number of companies are basing their price on the product's perceived value. . . . The company using perceived-value pricing must establish

the value in the buyers' minds concerning different
competitive offers.   —Principles of Marketing, *1983*[13]

Economic societies that are organized around the util-
itarian principle of imputed economic value should be
quite responsive in meeting the needs and wants of
society in ways that satisfy both consumers and producers. The incentive to produce highly valued goods
and services in cost effective ways is great. Penalties for
overproduction and inefficiency are real. If people do
indeed act principally out of self-interest, and economic
value is imputed by people to things, then there exists a
kinetic economic energy that will move economic activity toward market systems based on choice, with the objective of satisfying society's needs and wants. Even if
political institutions or other social institutions are created to mitigate against this force, it still exists as potential energy, like a bowling ball on a shelf ready to respond
to gravity.

In spite of all the advantages of markets, the fact remains that even in places where choice-based market
systems are most fully embraced, there are painful outcomes. It is possible to agree that people act out of self-
interest, that economic value is imputed, that economic
systems will naturally gravitate to coordination by choice
rather than by command, and yet look at the outcome
and conclude, "I don't like it!" Many people have reached
this conclusion and, by reason of philosophical commitment, believe economic values should be secondary to a
higher system of ethical or moral values. In answer to
these problems, they have turned to that outside-inside
definition of economic value based on a just price.

Justice, Just Prices, and Economic Value

> It is wholly sinful to practice fraud for the express purpose of selling a thing for more than its *just price*.
>
> —*St. Thomas Aquinas, 1273*[14]

> Again, there are some who sell their goods at a higher price than they command in the common market, or than is customary in the trade; and raise the price of their wares for no other reason than because they know that there is no more of that commodity in the country, or that the supply will shortly cease, and people must have it. . . . All such people are manifest thieves, robbers and usurers.
>
> —*Martin Luther, c. 1530*[15]

Although it is never really defined anywhere, the doctrine of a just price is applied whenever people are grieved by this world's economic injustices. A just price approach to economic value implies that all economic outcomes must be measured against a higher moral standard. If the economy falls short of that moral standard, the shortcoming must be addressed. Often people turn to government as the guardian of the public good, to step in and provide redress for economic wrongs. The degree to which government is called on to become involved will depend on the extent to which people in society believe there are wrongs to be righted. There is, as a result, a wide range of possibilities for the level of government involvement based on the varying degrees of economic injustice.

Justice has traditionally been applied to the realm of economics in three ways. First, exchanges should be fair; second, people should receive what they rightfully deserve; and third, economic rights as defined by society should be protected.

From the days of Aristotle to the present, society has recognized the injustice
stemming from situations where there
was a difference between what you
thought you were getting and what you
actually received. When the government
sets standards, inspects and grades food
products, legislates labeling requirements, or drafts truth-in-advertising, full-
disclosure-lending, and automobile
lemon laws, it is attempting to ensure that
what people actually receive in an exchange conforms to
what they thought they were getting.

We also see government intervention to ensure that people receive what they rightfully deserve.

★ ★ ★ ★ ★

We also see government intervention to ensure that
people receive what they rightfully deserve. It is this principle that is used to justify laws stating that

> Workers are entitled to a basic minimum wage.
> Workers are entitled to overtime pay (time and one-
> half) for work over 40 hours in a week.
> Workers are entitled to overtime pay for work over
> 8 hours in a day.
> Workers are entitled to be covered by workman's
> compensation insurance.
> Workers are entitled to unemployment insurance.
> Workers are entitled to 15 minutes of rest time for
> every 4 hours worked.
> Workers are entitled to a place of employment that
> is free from recognized hazards that are causing
> or are likely to cause death or serious injury.[16]

The requirements of this type of justice will depend on
how society defines the basic package of a person's rights.

To this package, many would like to add minimum retirement benefits, minimum holiday benefits, or minimum health-care benefits.

This same line of reasoning is sometimes used by developed nations to support import quotas and tariffs on agricultural products, automobiles, shoes, or anything else that would jeopardize the ability of its own workers in that industry to receive what they rightfully deserve. This affords workers in the developed country the opportunity to maintain a relatively high standard of living, while denying poorer workers in less-developed countries the chance to better their circumstances.

Our focus has been on the concept of economic value. Although this is different from moral values, they are not entirely unrelated. Moral values do become important considerations in measuring social justice. People can become quite uncomfortable with attempts to overlay the organization of economic activity with justice-seeking regulations. Those regulations will reflect an underlying system of values. When these values run counter to God's values, Christians will be reluctant to accept such regulation. The same can be said of those who oppose biblical values. They may be similarly reluctant to accept any attempt by Christians to impose their values on the organization of economic activity.

Prohibition of liquor and illicit drugs, restriction of pornography and gambling activities, laws against conducting business on Sundays, permissible discrimination in hiring practices based upon religious or sexual orientation, and laws restricting abortion are just a few examples of ways in which many Christians have been willing to overlay the free market with biblical values.

A Christian Response to Economic Value

Economic systems are social systems, and social systems are made up of people. But economic systems ultimately reduce themselves to the production and distribution of goods and services—"things," if you will. Things have no personality, no life, no rights, no soul. Things have no innate value. They only take on value as humans impute a value to them. Just as some would debate the question of whether a tree falling in the forest makes any sound, one could ask if things would have value if there were no people. But the question has little relevance for a world populated by human beings who consistently make choices about things in a way that they perceive will further their own interests, be they selfish or philanthropic.

There is a natural order to economic organization. Demand curves do slope down and to the right. People do pursue self-interest. People do prefer more rather than less. And yes, value is imputed based upon perceived utility. When it comes down to organizing economic activity, all of these principles must be taken into account. Democratic market economies are organized in harmony with these principles and have displayed a remarkable ability to produce things that people value.

> *People are more important than things, and sometimes the things people value run counter to a higher moral system of values that has been ordained by God.*
>
> ★ ★ ★ ★ ★

Christians, however, recognize that people are more important than things, and that sometimes the things people value run counter to a higher moral system of values that has been ordained by God. When the imputed value of things leads to a failure to meet human need, or when economic value imputed to things reflects a value system that is distorted by sin, then there is every reason to expect that not all of the outcomes of a free-market system will be pleasing to the Christian.

Many a call for a just price, a just wage, a just profit, a just output, comes from a recognition that systems based upon imputed values can produce flawed outcomes. As a result, a different value system is invoked, that of a just price. But these calls become problematic when attempts are made to substitute the "what should be" for the "what is." There "should be" a minimum wage. But minimum wages mean that some will go unemployed if they cannot create enough imputed value. People "should have" decent, affordable housing. But rent controls have a history of reducing the supply of housing and providing incentives that lead to the physical deterioration of what housing there is. People "should have" health care. But national health-care systems still lead to rationing in some form, even if it's based on something other than price.

Attempts to blindly overlay an economic world that is ordered by imputed values with a system of "should be" values are generally counterproductive. Beware of laws that attempt to accomplish, by rule, outcomes that will not be supported by the underlying values of society. Alexis de Tocqueville offered a similar warning when he said, "There is no country in which everything can be provided for by the laws, or in which political institutions can prove a substitute for common sense and public morality."[17]

On the other hand, Christians need to be careful to distinguish between culturally imputed values and the system of ultimate values ordained by God. Too great an acceptance of the former can lead to rejection of the latter. To see economic value as imputed is to accept the individual as the ultimate judge of value—in other words, to accept moral relativism. Right becomes whatever is right for you. There are no more absolutes. Is it any wonder Christians experience such hostility when they attempt to impose biblical standards of morality on a society immersed in an individually based system of value relativism? Externally imposed moral values strike at the very core of individual choice. This is nowhere more true than in a politically democratic, free-market system.

For example, people value the right to economic self-determination. But this right has contributed mightily to the cause of abortion on demand. The "cost" of any child includes giving up some measure of economic self-determination. Misguided supporters of abortion argue, "How can one be totally free to follow the full range of economic pursuits when encumbered with an unwanted child?" To bear a child is to incur economic sacrifice. When the cost is greater than the imputed value of a human life, then abortion becomes a rational choice. When the right to economic self-determination occupies a higher place in society's ranking of values than a human life does, then abortion on demand will make sense. It becomes a matter of *individual choice!*

Legalization of illicit drugs, pornography, prostitution, gambling, euthanasia, special privilege for immoral lifestyles are all the products of a corrupt system of values. The irony is that a free competitive market will do the best job of providing the highest "quality," lowest cost production and distribution of goods and services of this nature. *Markets are blind to any values other than those imputed to things.* Christians must recognize this fact.

One important principle to be aware of is that *market-based economic systems only reward people for the value of*

what they produce, not for their inherent value as persons.
Income redistribution can alleviate the problem only to the
extent that it does not destroy the incentive structures that
fuel the value-creating economic machine. But this too is
linked to society's system of values.

A more enduring response would include efforts to enable people to enter higher value-creating activities. This
gets more at the heart of the problem by admitting people
into the economic system and allowing them to reap rewards sufficient to lead a dignified life.

> **The outcomes of
> an economic
> system
> based upon the
> imputed values
> of a sinful world
> can run counter
> to values
> ordained by God.**
>
> ★ ★ ★ ★ ★

A proper understanding of the role of
imputed economic value should liberate
the Christian community to engage in a
more open dialogue on economic problems. It should be OK for Christians to talk
about *just price* sorts of issues without being labeled as antidemocratic or anti-
market extremists. Such discussion merely
reflects the reality that the outcomes of an
economic system based upon the imputed
values of a sinful world can run counter to
values ordained by God. On the other
hand, it does little good to organize eco-
nomic activity as if it were guided by just price concepts of
value, ignoring the fact that people make choices based
upon imputed values consistent with their own self-inter-
ests. To reject the market system based on imputed values is
to dam up the natural course of human endeavor.

So What Should I Do?

Market systems will do the best job of producing goods and
services that people want. What are we telling the market

we want? Show me your checkbook, and I'll tell you what you think is important in life. As an interesting exercise, you may want to make a list at the end of the year showing how you spent your money during the last twelve months. The results can be quite revealing.

When I was growing up, we learned a little song in Sunday school:

> *Be careful, little hands, what you do.*
> *Be careful, little hands, what you do.*
> *The Father up above is looking down in love.*
> *Oh, be careful, little hands, what you do.*

The other verses included "Be careful, little eyes, what you see," "Be careful, little feet, where you go," and "Be careful, little mouth, what you say." I would like to suggest that we add another verse: "Be careful, boys and girls, what you buy."

For not only is "the Father up above" interested in how we live our life, but there is also a vast and complex marketplace out there that is watching as well. That market is ever so eager for us to reveal what we truly value most in this world, and it stands ready to provide those things to us in a very efficient and effective manner.

As we have seen, in the real world value is imputed to things by people—including you and me. When you purchase a movie ticket, you are imputing value to the movie being shown and, in a larger sense, to the whole industry producing such films. What message have you just sent to the market? Is it a message that is consistent with your professed values?

When you buy a book or subscribe to cable TV packages, what does it say about what you value? How about your choices in clothing and food purchases? automobiles? vacations?

When we spend more and more on ourselves while the needs of others go unmet, what should the ever-watching marketplace conclude about what Christians value most?

We would all do well to remind ourselves that whenever we spend, there's a message we send. Consider carefully the choices you make.

Things Can Get Better

F ROM A DAD'S perspective, it had been a weary couple of days. Our family was suffering from the equivalent of a significant recession. Oh, it had nothing to do with a downturn in the family finances— even though it was the day before Christmas and we had the associated seasonal expenses. Our recession had a great deal more to do with the lack of harmonious relationships. These times tend to grab my attention, not because they represent the norm, but rather because they are the exception. And in this case, the last two days had really been exceptional.

It got to the point where all my fatherly wisdom had long since been expended, and all that was left was my fatherly frustration. I seized an opportunity, when there seemed to be some sign of a lull in the emotional mortar lobs, to call a family powwow. I began by asking, "What in the world is going on here? What has been happening to our family these last two days?"

We then went on to talk about a lot of the junk that had been going on, and it became clear that it was beyond us. Every single one of us agreed that the past two days had

161

been a mess, and we needed help. We needed to be rescued. It was a wonderful conclusion to reach the day before Christmas.

> The angel said to them, "Do not be afraid. I bring you good news of great joy that will be for all the people. Today in the town of David a Savior has been born to you; he is Christ the Lord." (Luke 2:10-11)

Every person in that family powwow had been a Christian for several years. We had all at one point been "saved." But recent events had impressed upon us how much we still needed God's help on a daily basis. In one sense, becoming "saved," the act of becoming a Christian, was indeed a one-time event. But in another sense, we need Christ the Savior to help us each day become more like him.

Becoming a Christian doesn't make you perfect. As long as we remain here on earth, we still have to deal with our sinful nature. But having a relationship with God provides the perspective, plan, and power for becoming better. Becoming better is a major part of what life is all about. God loves this world. He loves the people of this world. He has promised to, one day, make all things right. Although we must wait for him to totally fix all of the circumstances of life, he has promised to fix *us* now. He has also asked our help in bettering the conditions of this world.

DEVELOPING A CHRISTIAN PERSPECTIVE ON THE ECONOMY
Everyone admires the skill that a craftsman applies in the use of his trade, and we shudder at the thought of a dangerous instrument in the hands of the unskilled amateur. The novice will use it in inappropriate ways. *Credit* is a tool in a

modern, capitalistic economy. It can easily be misused and can serve to fuel an undisciplined appetite for spending. Christians should have the best credit records in a society, by virtue of learning to value things rightly, having the right priorities, and living a generally disciplined life. Christians should be the best examples of how, and how not, to use credit.

Property rights are at the core of a market system. Trading is a meaningless concept when you don't understand what is yours to trade. Property rights are protected by the authority of Scripture: "You shall not steal." The world works better when property rights are well defined and protected by law. Satan has, however, managed to distort the truth about property to the point that we too often act as if property were more valuable or more important than people. That is not the case, and we are well served to remind ourselves frequently of this error of humanity.

There is every reason to believe that Christians who engage in enterprise will find themselves in very profitable ventures. In a market economy, *profits* are the result of producing highly valued goods and services in cost-effective ways. Low-cost production means low use of scarce resources and good stewardship. Profit in enterprise can be entirely consistent with Christian principles.

Because we know that we are all still engaged in the process of becoming better, we can use all the help we can. *Competition* can act as a healthy force in our lives to motivate us to do better. It can serve to set a benchmark that allows us to measure ourselves against the standard of a successful competitor. Economic competition is the force that mitigates against extreme concentrations of power. All too often, the lack of competition in the economic sphere has led either to low-quality, lethargic, and unproductive uses of economic resources or to extreme and exploitive concentrations of economic power. As in the case of the profit motive, economic competition can further the best interests of society.

Government is an institution that Scripture acknowledges as having a legitimate role in the scope of human affairs. There are good reasons for limiting the role of government in areas where markets can serve the needs of society. Because of the potential for imperfection, government institutions and people serving in the government sector are in special need of the Christian's prayer support. These institutions seem particularly vulnerable and are well served by our attention to prayer. But just as governments will not always be perfect, neither will markets, and therein lies another justification for the existence of government.

Getting better also means living with our *personal finances* under control. When this dimension of life is in balance, giving, saving, and maintaining a disciplined standard of living will be a part of our life.

Credit, consumers, profits, competition, and private property are all part of what it means to have a market economy. But is a market economy a Christian economy? No. No economic system is "Christian"; only people can be Christians. So where do Christians go for solutions to economic problems?

Part of the answer is, I believe, the market system. It is without a doubt the most effective and efficient means of producing goods and services. The best long-term solutions to problems of economic hardship will be those that first recognize imputed value as the operational force in guiding economic activity and then work to incorporate this in the solution. An example would be looking for ways to make a low-skilled worker more productive in the value-creating process instead of legislating minimum wages, which have the effect of eliminating employment opportunities.

Another part of the answer to economic problems is the state. Look to the state to support and promote the democratic capitalist market structure. Look to the state to correct market shortcomings, such as those stemming from unreasonable concentrations of market power or from societal costs or benefits that might be external to a given market. Look to the state to provide public goods, such as national defense, law enforcement, highway systems, national and state parks. Look to the state, as custodian of the common good, to facilitate income redistribution without sacrificing future welfare by destroying value-creating incentives. Whenever you look to the state, be sure any proffered solution submits to the constraints of economic choice as it is practiced in reality.

And finally, the church needs to be part of the answer to economic problems. The church must be salt and light in a world of decay and darkness. Look to the church to provide, by both voice and example, moral restraint; for liberty without moral restraint is nothing more than license. Look to the church to model the ultimate and eternal values ordained by God. Look to the people of the church to respond individually and collec-

I am skeptical of attempts by the church to impose the full range of a Christian, biblical value system on a world that now looks to the individual as the supreme judge of value. The world hated Jesus for doing just that, and they will appreciate us no more than they did him.

★ ★ ★ ★ ★

tively to the physical as well as spiritual needs of mankind. Look for the people of God to exert their personal influence wherever possible, to achieve outcomes that are economically good and just.

I am skeptical of attempts by the church to impose the full range of a Christian, biblical value system on a world that now looks to the individual as the supreme judge of value. The world hated Jesus for doing just that, and they will appreciate us no more than they did him. But look to the true church of Jesus Christ to spread the gospel of personal salvation, which offers life-transforming power to people of every walk of life who choose to accept the Word. If the people of this world were to willingly subject their own personal will to God's will, we would have little to fear from a system of imputed values, for it would flow from the values of God himself.

> **Things can get better. Christianity offers a perspective on economic issues that can lead to a better world.**
>
> ★ ★ ★ ★ ★

There will no doubt be days when you look around at the way life has been going and conclude, much as I did at home that Christmas Eve, that things are a mess. No economic system, no government, not even the church will provide the perfect solution to the economic dilemmas of life. That is why we need a Savior. The answers to many of our problems cannot be found within the context of this world. The answers lie in the eternal dimension of God, not bound by time or locked in space or limited by the resources of this world. But God has come to us. We know him as Jesus.

We often think about how Christianity can make our personal life better. We frequently apply it to the context of family and church. We consider it in the context of missions and general ministry as well. But because economic activity is so integral to modern life, I believe it is important to also spend time considering how Christianity relates to this sphere of human endeavor. It's important to realize that there is a Savior who stands ready to act even in the context of economic activity.

And because of that, there is hope. Things can get better. Christianity offers a perspective on economic issues that can lead to a better world.

NOTES

Introduction. The Good Old Days

1. *Statistical Abstract of the United States, 1994*, 87.
2. Ibid., 403.
3. Stanley Lebergott, *Pursuing Happiness: American Consumers in the Twentieth Century* (Princeton University Press, 1993), 51.
4. Ibid., 95–107.
5. Ibid. 112.
6. *Statistical Abstract of the United States, 1994*, 15, 179.

Chapter 1. Reasons to Believe

1. *Information Please Almanac, 1994*, 127.
2. *World Almanac, 1993*, 132; *World Almanac, 1994*, 112.
3. *World Resources, 1991–1992*, 273.
4. *World Almanac & Book of Facts, 1994*, 128.
5. Supt. of Documents, *Survey of Current Business* 73 (Washington, D.C.: GPO, August 1993), 56.
6. *World Almanac, 1994*, 822; *Information Please Almanac, 1994*, 128.
7. *World Almanac, 1994*, 822.
8. *Statistical Abstract of the United States, 1994*, 114th ed., 823–824.
9. Ibid., 800–801.
10. McKinsey Global Institute, "Manufacturing Productivity," quoted in *The Economist*, 23 October 1993, 88. The study focused on data from 1990.
11. *Economic Report of the President, 1992*, 91.
12. "More Than Meets the Eye," *The Economist*, 26 December 1993, 91.
13. "More Than Meets the Eye," *The Economist*, 26 December 1993, 91, quoting Michael Darby, "Causes of Declining Growth" in Federal

Reserve Bank of Kansas City symposium on "Policies for Long-Run Economic Growth," 1992.

14. *World Almanac, 1994,* 822; 766; 819.
15. *World Resources, 1992–1993,* 305.
16. *World Almanac, 1994,* 128.
17. *World Resources, 1992–1993,* 144; 314.
18. *World Almanac, 1994,* 155.
19. Ibid., 155; *World Resources, 1992–1993,* 149.
20. *Statistical Abstract of the United States, 1993,* 477. The stock of capital in 1991, net of depreciation, was estimated at $15,412 billion, approximately $60,000 per capita.
21. *World Resources, 1992–1993,* 266.
22. Ibid., 266–267.
23. Ibid.
24. Ibid., 266.
25. Ibid.
26. Ibid.
27. *World Almanac, 1993,* 178–179.
28. *Science & Engineering Indicators, 1991,* 10th ed., 402–404.
29. *Science & Engineering, 1991,* 389. Data compiled by the National Science Board.
30. James A. Wilcox, *Current Readings on Money, Banking, & Financial Markets* (New York: HarperCollins College, 1989), 228.
31. *Newsweek,* 21 January 1991, 8.
32. *Economic Report of the President, 1993,* 423.
33. Schiller, *Macro Economy,* 40. This calculation was based on the price deflator for gross domestic product 1930–1992 (1987=100). The original source was the Department of Commerce, Bureau of Economic Analysis.
34. Schiller, *Macro Economy,* 121.
35. *Federal Reserve Bulletin,* March 1994.
36. Ibid.
37. "Doleful," *The Economist,* 9 October 1993, 17.
38. Much of the information about the European labor market has been drawn from David Henderson, "The Europeanization of the U.S. Labor Market," *The Public Interest* 113, Fall 1993, 66–81.
39. Henderson, "U.S. Labor Market," 73.
40. *Statistical Abstract, 1993,* 408.
41. Greg J. Duncan et al., *Years of Poverty, Years of Plenty* (Ann Arbor: Ann Arbor Institute of Social Research, 1984).
42. *Statistical Abstract, 1993* (using data from 1988), 850.
43. Ibid.

44. "Training for Jobs," *The Economist,* 12 March 1994, 26.
45. *Statistical Abstract, 1993,* 477. Actual estimates for the net value of tangible wealth at the end of 1992 were not as yet available from the Bureau of Labor and Statistics. The year-end 1992 number of $16 trillion was arrived at by taking available 1991 data ($15.4 trillion) and extrapolating to 1992. The net stock of the nation's structures and equipment has been increasing at an average annual compound rate of 4.6 percent from 1982 to 1991.
46. *Survey of Current Business,* August 1993, 71.
47. *Economic Report of the President, 1993,* 348, using GDP of $5.98 trillion and net interest of $187.1 billion.
48. *Survey of Current Business,* August 1993, 62.
49. Ibid.
50. Lawrence H. Summers, "The Challenges of Development: Some Lessons of History for Sub-Saharan Africa, International Monetary Fund and the World Bank," *Finance and Development,* March 1992, 7–9.
51. Summers, "The Challenges of Development," March 1992, 7.

Chapter 2. Lending for Spending—
It Just Might Be the Neighborly Thing to Do

1. This example uses an 18 percent interest rate, which is a common rate for revolving consumer credit and credit cards.

Chapter 3. Mind Your "Mines"

1. Lloyd Timberlake, *Africa in Crisis* (London & Washington, D.C.: Earthscan/International Institute for Environment and Development, 1985), 116–117, 120–121.
2. P. J. Hill, "Environmental Problems under Socialism" (paper presented at Mont Perlin Society Meeting, Big Sky, Montana, August 22–26, 1991). The paper was subsequently accepted for publication in the CATO Journal.

Chapter 5. It's a Jungle Out There

1. William M. Corley, "Fare Game: Did Northwest Steal American's Systems?" *Wall Street Journal,* 7 July 1994, A1:6.

Chapter 6. Should the Word *Government* Be Capitalized?

1. See *Economic Report of the President, 1992,* 141.

Chapter 7. Getting a Grip on Your Finances

1. See *Merriam-Webster's Collegiate Dictionary,* 10th ed., s.v. "greed."
2. Ibid., "acquisitiveness."

3. The study was conducted by Empty Tomb, Inc., a Christian research group in Champaign, Illinois. Some results were reported in the *Kane County (Illinois) Chronicle*, 28 September 1993.

4. *Wall Street Journal*, 11 October 1990.

Chapter 8. What Is It Worth?

1. Cannan, Edwin, "The Theory of Value in General," *A Review of Economic Theory* (London: Frank Cass and Co., 1929), 154.

2. Psalm 90:17

3. Colossians 3:23-24

4. John Milton, *Paradise Lost*, book 4, lines 618–20.

5. Cotton Mather, "A Christian and His Calling," in *Puritanism and the American Experience*, ed. Michael McGiffert (Redding, Mass.: Addison-Wesley, 1969), 122–127.

6. Charles F. Harrold and William D. Templeman, eds., "Past and Present" in *English Prose of the Victorian Era*, (New Oxford University Press, 1938), quoted in Leland Ryken, *Work & Leisure—A Christian Perspective* (Portland, Ore.: Multnomah Press, 1987), 74.

7. Harold D. Lehman, *In Praise of Leisure* (Scottdale, Penn.: Herald Press, 1974), quoted in Leland Ryken, *Work & Leisure—A Christian Perspective* (Portland, Oreg.: Multnomah Press, 1987), 25.

8. Sidney Davidson and Roman Weil, *Handbook of Modern Accounting*, 3rd ed. (New York: McGraw Hill, 1983), 38-16–38-17.

9. Philip Kotler, *Marketing Management*, 5th ed. (Englewood Cliffs, N.J.: Prentice-Hall, 1984), 516–17.

10. Victor P. Buell, ed., *Handbook of Modern Marketing*, (New York: McGraw Hill, 1896), 30-2–30-3.

11. Carl Menger, *A Theory of Value* (Found Class Reprints, 1984), quoted in *Source Readings in Economics*, 359–60.

12. Peter Drucker, *Management, Tasks, Responsibilities, Practices* (New York: Harper & Row, 1973) 84–85.

13. Philip Kotler, *Principles of Marketing*, 2nd ed. (Englewood Cliffs, N.J.: Prentice-Hall, 1983), 329.

14. St. Thomas, *"Summa Theologica,"* in *History of Economic Thought: A Book of Readings*, ed. Kapp & Kapp (New York: Barnes & Noble, 1956), 7–8.

15. Martin Luther, "On Trading and Usury," in *History of Economic Thought: A Book of Readings*, ed. Kapp & Kapp (New York: Barnes & Noble, 1956), 25.

16. Section 119 of the Occupational Safety and Hazard Act.

17. Alexis de Tocqueville, *Democracy in America*, book 1, chapter 8.